DEEP LESSONS ON COLLABORATION

Editors:

Patrick Sanaghan
Nancy Aronson

Contributors:

Nancy Aronson
Francis E. Blanco
Susan Felker
Samuel Frisby
Jeffrey Marshall
Joan Reilly
Patrick Sanaghan
Amy Steffen
Lonnie Weiss
Sharon Young

Published by:

DEEP LESSONS ON COLLABORATION

How Collaboration Really Works

Edited by

Patrick Sanaghan and Nancy Aronson

Library of Congress Control Number: 2009903007
ISBN: Hardcover   978-1-4415-2424-9
                   Softcover   978-1-4415-2423-2

This book was printed in the United States of America.

To order additional copies of this book, contact:
Xlibris Corporation
1-888-795-4274
www.Xlibris.com
Orders@Xlibris.com
54016

CONTENTS AND SUMMARY

I. Introduction 9

II. Changing Attitudes and Breaking Stereotypes:
    Mobilizing Action in Education 11

Providing high-quality educational opportunities is one of the most important responsibilities of a society. This case study describes how a pivotal collaborative strategic planning event and the resulting partnerships helped change negative attitudes and stereotypes toward vocational education. North Montco Technical Career Center, in Lansdale, Pennsylvania, once on the brink of closing, is now having a positive regional impact.

These are its unique characteristics:

- The use of a particular methodology, a Future Search, to mobilize the whole system
- The role of leadership in opening up a system
- Making the most of a mandated state requirement

III. Revitalizing Neighborhood Parks: An Arranged
     Marriage Leads to Transformation............................ 22

The Pennsylvania Horticultural Society (PHS) and the Philadelphia Department of Recreation (PDR) have been involved in a fifteen-year collaborative relationship that is an extraordinary example of how a city organization, with its complexities and hierarchies, can work with a nonprofit organization to serve the greater good. This partnership has been at the core of reclaiming neighborhood parks throughout Philadelphia. It has stood the test of time and endured the transition of top leaders in both organizations. It now stands as a comprehensive and intelligent model for building communities in our urban areas. This case study spells out what it takes to preserve relationships, continuity, energy, and enthusiasm over time.

These are its unique characteristics:

- Sustaining a partnership over time
- Building a comprehensive program from a small-scale initiative
- How the little things are big things in relationship building

IV. Cultivating New Resources 34

In 2003, Secretary Michael DiBerardinis created an inclusive, participative planning process that meaningfully engaged over 1,800 internal and external stakeholders of the Pennsylvania Department of Conservation and Natural Resources (DCNR). Disciplined, flexible, and outcomes based, this planning process did not start with conclusions but was open to input from others. The ideas, criticisms, and passions of many citizens helped create the DCNR Action Plan. This plan focused the efforts, attention, resources, and decision making of an entire state department. This case study details how to create and implement a large-scale collaborative planning process.

These are its unique characteristics:

- Entry process for a new leader
- Large-scale engagement
- Building internal capacity

V. The Road to Collaboration 46

The New Jersey Department of Transportation (NJDOT) conducted an environmental impact study (EIS) to find a roadway solution for a highly congested area of the state. Interest groups had blocked an earlier recommendation from proceeding forward. This second effort involved mayors from four municipalities, environmental advocacy groups, neighborhood and merchants associations, state agencies, and major landowners in the study area. There were a number of hot issues. Decision makers used a facilitated, collaborative, multifaceted process to develop a recommendation, and the NJDOT made the final decision. It was not challenged by a lawsuit—a grand success for the department!

These are its unique characteristics:

- Structures and processes for managing a complex, conflict-laden situation
- An alternative to public hearings as a decision-making forum

- The role of leader as protector of the integrity of the process
- A story of participative democracy

VI. The SCOOP Initiative 60

In 2001, the mayor of Trenton, New Jersey, convened a youth summit to discuss the possibility of creating an integrated youth network. The City of Trenton Department of Recreation, Natural Resources, and Culture and the Trenton School District hosted this summit, involving over one hundred service providers.

As a result, the Social Celebrations, Organizations, Opportunities and People initiative (SCOOP) was created to provide high-quality after-school programs for youth; strategies for dealing with at-risk youth; ways to build cross-boundary partnerships with clergy, business, and higher education; and, most importantly, a coherent and integrated service system for young people. Today, over three thousand students participate in one hundred-plus programs at twenty-seven sites across the city. The creation of SCOOP involved public and private partnerships, unions, politicians, and funders and required an unprecedented level of collaboration.

These are its unique characteristics:

- Structures that enable collaboration across seemingly self-contained departments
- What it means to bring the "right" people to the table
- Effective use of political power

VII. Nature under Pressure 72

Lasting Landscapes is a comprehensive, collaborative approach to conserving natural resources that are highly valued by their communities for their scientific or historical significance. Whether a bird sanctuary or a revolutionary war site, these natural resources help provide a *sense of place* for a community. The Lasting Landscapes approach helps a community coalesce interest and energy around the preservation and sustainability of these resources. The approach has been used in seven settings with impressive results. This chapter illustrates the basics of the Lasting Landscapes approach and its application in a variety of environments.

These are its unique characteristics:

- An effective blending of outside technical expertise and inside community expertise
- Using a community-based approach
- Implementing and replicating a theoretically sound, practically tested model

VIII. Conclusion.. 83

How this Book is Organized

The book contains six case studies, many of which involve our natural resources. We have included others that do not because we wanted to see if there were any common guiding principles or embedded lessons across very different kinds of collaborative work. Some of the case studies explore finished work while others examine work in progress. Each case study has a section on lessons learned. You can pick and choose or read from beginning to end. All offer important perspectives that we hope will inform your thinking. The concluding chapter includes observations from across the cases. Read on and see what we found. Enjoy the journey!

I. INTRODUCTION

I S IT REALLY possible to solve thorny, complex problems where competing interests are so strong and so deep that finding a solution seems beyond reach? Is it possible to create substantive programs for youth in an underserved, underresourced urban environment? Is it possible to change long-held negative stereotypes of vocational education so more students have options and opportunities for success? Can a forced marriage between two very different organizations work over the long term to revitalize community assets? Is it possible for a state agency to listen to all of its stakeholders and evolve its leadership role and create future strategies?

The answer is yes! The case studies in this book provide examples of organizations and communities reaching new levels of collaboration to accomplish the seemingly impossible.

What You Can Learn about Collaboration

If we are to effectively manage the critical and complex issues facing our society, we must understand the crucial role collaboration plays in our work and social lives. To deal with tough, overwhelming issues like youth violence, education, and the environment, we must learn to collaborate across traditional boundaries, both within our organizations and across our communities.

These cases reveal the wisdom of collaboration in challenging circumstances. The challenges come from the scale or complexity of the effort, the political environment, or the fact that the issue being addressed is for the common good but not necessarily part of the explicit agenda for any one organization. This monograph focuses on *what works*. We believe these are portable lessons that can be applied to a wide variety of situations, particularly those that require people to work across boundaries of departments, functions, organizations, and communities. Many of us know we have to partner with others to achieve results, but we are not sure how. The monograph provides some concrete answers.

Why is collaboration so important right now? We propose that as a society (and a world), we are reaching the limits of our well-intentioned, uncoordinated activities. We can no longer take piecemeal, compartmentalized approaches to difficult, systemic issues. We need to learn how to share power, ideas, and resources. For example, think of all the organizations and agencies in a community that attend, in some way, to the natural environment. Now imagine if they coordinated their activities, leveraged their resources, and worked together. If we are to preserve what is important to our communities, we have to learn to combine our strengths.

We're living in a time when many observe that civil discourse is on the decline. Partisanship and individual self-interest are commonplace in public arenas. To reconcile deeply held positions and conflicting agendas, we must learn to collaborate at deeper levels and provide more opportunities for dialogue. Civic engagement and participation are critical ingredients to a vibrant democracy. Civil discourse involves knowing your voice counts; creating opportunities for differences to be aired and explored; and discovering common aspirations among your colleagues, potential partners, or neighbors. The cases in this monograph offer approaches for constructive, powerful civic engagement.

The purpose of this monograph is to build hope and show possibility. The authors include both insiders (i.e., middle- and upper-level organizational leadership) and outsiders (i.e., consultants). This professional mix adds to the richness of these collaborative cases. External consultants bring the theories, frameworks, and processes at fifty thousand feet. Insiders bring the know-how, are relationship savvy, and understand the practical applications at ground level.

Who Should Read this Monograph?

This is a *practitioner's* book. It is written for individuals and leaders who want to learn about the complexities of collaboration. This is for people who want to expand their choices for managing important issues constructively. We want to support and inform the courageous people who undertake this difficult and hopeful work.

II. CHANGING ATTITUDES AND BREAKING STEREOTYPES

Mobilizing Action in Education

Nancy Aronson

Challenge: How a collaborative effort helped turn around a failing vocational-technical school

Introduction

WHEN A NEW executive director took over the North Montgomery County Area Vo-Tech School north of Philadelphia in 1993, he found an organization facing serious problems. The year before, the five local school districts, which sent students to this vo-tech school and underwrote it financially, had wanted to close the school. In addition to being held in low regard by other educators, the school suffered from common negative stereotypes associated with vocational-technical education:

- The school was a dumping ground for problem students or low achievers.
- Vocational education was for nonacademic students.
- Some parents who attended the vo-tech school in the 1970s remember it having a drug culture—a stigma that it still held almost thirty years later.
- Industry viewed the school as out of touch with local labor needs.

The staff was talented, but morale was low, and they had little hope for the future. If an organization could be said to have low self-esteem, this one had it.

Fast Forward: 2002

By the beginning of the 2002-2003 school year, the image of the school had improved, and the situation was dramatically different. The school evolved from a traditional vo-tech to a technical career center. A new name for the school, North Montco Technical Career Center, reflected both the changes and the school's new image. The school had a renewed sense of vitality and possibility. Enrollment went from 420 in 1992 to 1,300 just ten years later, and there was a waiting list too. Gains were made in the areas of academic achievement, and there were high expectations for students. The educational and technical opportunities for students were expanded. Teachers were exhibiting tremendous initiative in both their own professional growth as well as in continually developing and refining high-quality courses for students.

Math and reading achievement scores, as measured by standardized achievement scores on statewide tests, increased significantly for students taught reading and math skills within the context of their technical training. Specifically, the average scores for these students were up 200 points on these tests versus other technical students who were taught math and reading in their home schools—traditional comprehensive high schools.

Technical students were taking more challenging and rigorous academic courses. For example, in the past, machine-shop students were not required to take specific, higher academic courses and would take general math. Today, students who want to be machinists take geometry, trigonometry, and calculus. The school has established pathways with rigorous academic courses for all program areas.

The school is distinguished by the ability of students to take either a technical or academic path. The school formalized over forty articulation agreements with two-year and four-year colleges across the state. This means that these colleges give advanced credit for course work taken at the technical school to students who elect to continue their studies at the postsecondary level. This eliminates redundant course work and enables students to take more advanced or elective courses in college. Engineering technology students could receive up to fifteen college credits for fundamental technology classes taken in high school when they matriculate into a community college technology program.

High standards have also been infused into the technical aspects of the school. The school has access to state-of-the-art equipment and provides high-quality training and hands-on experiences for students.

Teachers have been very active in advancing the programs and offerings for students. For example, teachers in the power and transportation cluster worked to get their programs nationally certified through Automotive Service Excellence (ASE). This is the same certification found in the "real world." Perhaps the most dramatic display of teacher leadership occurred when teachers organized themselves to apply for and receive International Standards Operation (ISO) certification. This certification is a well-known and well-respected status marker in the national and international community. ISO certification signals that this organization "actually does what it purports to do."

Factors for Success

These are just a few examples of substantive changes made at this school. What factors contributed to this success?

The new executive director led the school in initially taking small steps and then "opened" up the organization to new levels of collaboration with others. He believed that this openness would lead to new possibilities and encourage other stakeholders to take initiative on behalf of the school. As energy and optimism grew, ideas were put into action. In describing the journey, a number of factors will be highlighted. The first has to do with the attributes of the executive director.

A Realistic and Optimistic Leader

The executive director deeply believed that most of the staff were talented and committed. He also knew the school had a serious image problem. He understood the complexity of having a board made up of representatives from the five sending school districts. He was also committed to the importance of technical education and the opportunities it could provide students on a regional basis. He held both a tough-minded view of the current reality and a sense of possibility. He knew that rebuilding trust with the sending schools and the community was essential. Most of the staff understood that the school's future was in question, and they were willing to do some things differently.

Small Steps Begin to Build Momentum

Youth apprenticeships were created to augment in-class learning with relevant on-the-job experiences. These well-received programs were important first steps in the school's evolution into a contemporary, viable technical career center. A name change, to the North Montgomery County Technical Career Center (NMTCC or the Career Center), marked this aspiration and sent a signal that business would not be continuing in the usual ways. The stage was set for the next pivotal event: mandated strategic planning.

Strategic Planning—the School Leaps Forward

In 1996, the executive director, his assistant director, and a team of teachers met to discuss how the school should approach state-mandated strategic planning. The consultants encouraged them to be *strategic* about strategic planning. The group determined that they wanted to do more than just fulfill the requirements; they wanted this planning process to be a pivotal experience in the life of the school. Positive changes had begun with the youth apprenticeship program, and the timing was right. They believed there was now enough hope and interest in the school—enough initial momentum—to ask people to commit their time and energy to creating a better future.

Making Mandates Meaningful

A Future Search was chosen as the primary approach to strategic planning. A Future Search is a sixteen- to twenty-hour meeting held over three days with sixty-four to one hundred people, representing the whole system. Its basic principles include opening up the system, particularly bringing all voices into the room to be part of the planning. This was essential to the executive director. This highly engaging, participative process yields a shared vision; common-ground goals; and, in this case, possibilities for action. It is built upon the following principles:

- *Get the whole system in the room.* The whole system means diverse internal stakeholders (such as teachers and administrators) and external stakeholders (such as sending school administrators and teachers, parents, business partners, students)—anyone with information, authority, resources, expertise, and a stake in the future of the organization. Having the whole system in the room helps people make decisions on behalf of the whole instead of narrow interests. It also enhances the action possibilities and increases the potential of the system.
- *Explore the whole before focusing on fixing any part.* When people share what they know, all gain an understanding of the whole that none had coming in. Actions are taken within a shared frame of reference.

- *Keep the future and common ground front and center.* Acknowledge the past, acknowledge the present, and focus on the future. Problems and conflicts become information to share, not action items. The agenda is a search for shared goals and mutually supported plans to achieve them.
- *Invite self-management and responsibility for action.* Groups can often do much more than is asked of them. Active engagement is encouraged. Each time a leader or consultant does the work of the group, it slows down ownership and responsibility for everyone else.

Live Your Future Now

In addition to producing concrete outcomes, the principles and characteristics of a Future Search modeled what this organization wanted to accomplish in *relationship* to its larger community. It allowed the school to immediately open up the system, engage people in meaningful dialogue, and change the negative impressions of the school in real time as people worked together on important tasks related to the school's future. From the planning of the Future Search conference to postconference activities, strong signals were sent that this was a new day.

Planning the Future Search Conference

A steering group was formed to help shape the conference. Although a Future Search conference has particular tasks—exploring the past, assessing the present, creating desired future scenarios, discovering common ground, and action planning, the role of the steering group was critical in the following:

- Clarifying the purpose of the conference (beyond meeting a state mandate)
- Inviting the right mix of people to achieve this purpose, and
- Tailoring the activities to meet the specific needs of the school.

The twelve people on the steering group were a mix of the school's internal and external stakeholders. Right from the start, representatives from the sending schools, potential business partners, parents, and students were sitting with faculty and administration making collaborative decisions.

This group developed a theme for the conference, "Innovative Approaches to Unlocking the Future," and articulated its purposes. This theme was chosen very carefully. The steering group wanted to invite people to dream and *really* think outside of the box. They also wanted to communicate that this was about creating the future of the school, not looking to the past to fix old mistakes. The energy was forward moving. The three purposes the steering group articulated for the conference were as follows:

- Set the directions for the future of NMTCC as part of the strategic planning process.
- Acquire and share information through the interaction of representatives of nine stakeholder groups.
- Expand and strengthen relationships among NMTCC, its sending schools, local businesses, and community members.

The steering group took great care in determining the right mix of people to invite to the conference. They wanted people with information, influence, and resources. They wanted a mix that would provide a full picture of the past and current reality of vocational education in the county plus accelerate the action possibilities for the school. A key member of the steering group was an executive from a large company, a parent of an honors student, and a deep believer in technical education. Through his international contacts, he invited a partner from a technical school in Germany, a country that is a world leader in apprenticeship programs, to attend the Future Search.

The members of the steering committee took two important steps in securing conference participation. They made personal contacts to encourage attendance, and they insisted that invitees attend all three days. The activities and decisions of the steering committee sent a strong message to the network of stakeholders about the importance of this meeting.

The Future Search Is a Pivotal Event

The Future Search, although only a three-day meeting, was a pivotal event in the life of the school. The conference yielded seven strategic goals for the school:

1. *Career education.* To utilize all resources to achieve ongoing career education from kindergarten through adulthood

2. *Curriculum.* To design an educational program of high standards compatible with changing needs of students and employers, involving full use of all available resources
3. *Facility.* To maximize all available resources to meet clients' needs
4. *Global interconnections.* To bring the world together through cultural, technological, and business exchange, i.e., global learning
5. *Individual educational needs.* To meet individual educational needs by using all learning options
6. *Partnerships.* To strengthen partnerships with postsecondary education, parents, students, business/industry, government, community agencies, and home schools in order to enhance training for all students
7. *Technology.* To develop a process that anticipates change while staying current through creative use of technology

The goals were relevant to the school and also were a key component of the plan submitted to the Pennsylvania Department of Education. NMTCC effectively managed the often-competing interests of organizational relevance and state or federal government compliance. Opening up the system and getting the relevant stakeholders together to discuss the future of vocational-technical education in the region had a major impact on the system. It created a climate of possibility and led to many concrete programs.

During the conference, the faculty became energized as they listened to participants from business talk about *what-ifs*. "What if we came to the school site and partnered with faculty to do training?" "What if we brought students to our work sites and gave them experience on leading-edge equipment that would be too expensive for the school to own?" The what-ifs offered exciting possibilities and communicated an interest in the school. As one participant described, "The energy was magic." Many of these what-ifs became reality. The partnerships formed and the relationships built paid dividends for many years to come. Here are some examples:

- When a major automotive equipment manufacturer consigned $150,000 worth of its products to the school's automotive lab, students had the opportunity to be trained on the same equipment found in modern automotive-dealership service departments. The manufacturer benefited too because they were able to bring potential buyers to the school where the equipment was in use. This type of business-education partnership goes far beyond the more typical setup of businesses giving schools used or slightly outdated equipment. This is a mutual, win-win partnership.

- In partnership with major pharmaceutical firms, a biotechnology lab was established in the school to serve both high school students and adults. Imagine students receiving training alongside their industry counterparts!

Parents communicated a very strong message that they wanted their children to have the choice to pursue a *technical* path or an *academic* path. The school listened. The dual importance of technical skills and academics has become a signature of the school.

Prior to the conference, teachers talked about having too many things on their plates. Does this sound familiar? An additional by-product of the Future Search was a shift in how teachers viewed current initiatives and new activities. Although their workload remained the same, by seeing the bigger picture, experiencing the larger context, and hearing from other stakeholders, the teachers could make connections and better understand how all the pieces fit together. There was a palpable emotional shift in how teachers viewed their work and how much energy they expended to make new things happen.

Maintaining Momentum

After the Future Search, the school did a number of things to sustain the energy and momentum:

- Ad hoc teams replaced standing committees. As priorities and issues arose around a goal area, ad hoc teams with appropriate stakeholders were formed, the priority or issue was addressed, and the group was disbanded when the work was completed. This may sound routine, however, in education (and other arenas), you can get "standing committee-itis." Planning fatigue can set in, or people can begin to confuse planning with taking action.
- As these ad hoc teams were formed, the question was continually asked, who needs to be in the room? This supported the principle of planning *with* others, not *for* others. This principle accelerates implementation.
- A public review meeting was held twenty-four months after the Future Search. Participants were invited back to share successes and

challenges and to chart progress. New ideas and possibilities were also discussed.

Lessons Learned

A Few People Can Make a Big Difference

A few deeply committed people can create opportunities for others to engage and make meaningful contributions. For example, one of the parents wanted his son, an honors student at the high school, to be able to go to this school. He believed that technical schools could be highly valued, superior places for learning. Along with the executive director, he was a driving force behind the conference. He was an active member of the steering committee where he used his considerable influence to bring others to the table, including a colleague from Germany.

Courageous Leadership

Bringing the whole system together to shape the future requires a willingness to lead without having all the answers. Leaders expend a good deal of capital bringing people together in this way, particularly if this kind of whole-system work goes against the prevailing cultural norms of the organization or the field. For example, education is often considered an expert-driven field. Leaders are expected to have the answer, and they often employ strategies that emphasize acceptance of predetermined outcomes and overcoming resistance to change. Collaboration and shared decision making takes courage on the part of leaders. It also contributes to deeper ownership on the part of others and breakthroughs in what can happen. The new executive director, Mike Erwin, was just the type of catalytic, courageous leader the organization needed. He brought an entrepreneurial spirit and deep commitment to opening up the system. His leadership, combined with a strategic, systematic collaborative process, got the system on a new road; and the school had the assets—committed, talented teachers—to sustain it.

Critical Issues Become System Opportunities

The issues facing NMTCC were critical, and the level of dissatisfaction with the school was cause for great concern. The future of the school was at risk, but this fact alone was not enough to propel the school toward the needed transformational changes. A planning process that *acknowledges* the past and present and focuses on the *future* allowed the system to create and redirect the energy constructively.

In this case, the Future Search was able to build on the positive momentum that begun with the youth apprenticeship programs and leverage it exponentially. The school not only complied with the state-mandated strategic planning process; it used it as an opportunity to do something meaningful in the life of the organization.

Planning for Desired Future Relationships

As part of the strategic planning effort, the school wanted to shift their relationships with external stakeholders. It wanted to open the system up to more collaboration and deeper partnerships. The school started modeling this stance from the beginning. A diverse steering group made up of internal and external stakeholders shaped the Future Search conference by articulating the purpose and inviting participants. They worked with the facilitators to tailor conference activities so they would be meaningful to *all* the different stakeholder groups.

If one of the desired outcomes is increased partnership, get the partners in the room thinking with you. This allows planning *with*, not *for* other people. At this conference, it wasn't just faculty discussing what they would want business and industry partners to do for them; the partners and potential partners were at the table. The planning processes that organizations or communities choose are fateful. If increased collaboration is an aspiration, choose a process that models that.

During the action-planning phase of the conference, participants identified initiatives or programs they wanted to launch and had an opportunity to begin making plans with other like-minded people. It was not a planning-for-planning's-sake process. Once again, it modeled planning *with* others, not *for* others. The system continued to link planning and action with its use of ad hoc teams addressing priority issues as they arose. "Following the energy" leads to results.

A Story of Hope

The story of NMTCC inspires hope on two levels. One is that an organization is actually able to transform its image in the marketplace and community. The fact that the school was able to reverse a downward spiral makes it possible for other organizations facing similar challenges to do the same. The school also inspires hope for education. Its programs offer viable, relevant, engaging educational opportunities for students. Depending on their aspirations, students are ready for work and ready for college. This can serve as a model for other schools interested in engaging all types of learners and preparing them for the world of work or the world of higher education.

Nancy Aronson is a partner with Arsht/Aronson. You can contact her at *naronson1@cs.com.*

Resources

- Weisbord, M. and S. Janoff. *Future Search: An Action Guide to Finding Common Ground in Organizations and Communities.* 2nd ed. San Francisco: Berrett-Kohler, 2000.
- http://www.futuresearch.net

III. REVITALIZING CITY PARKS

An Arranged Marriage Leads to Urban Transformation

Joan Reilly

Challenge: To build a citywide partnership to revitalize and transform neglected parks

Introduction

HOW ARE A neighborhood and city affected when their parks are neglected? Open spaces that are treasured and maintained are true community assets, but when neglected, these same spaces become real liabilities. At best, they are eyesores. At worst, they become havens for illegal activity that thrives in the cover of darkness and neglect and preys on the life of a community. Drug dealing, substance abuse, prostitution, truancy, and illegal dumping all prosper in this type of situation. And in the city of Philadelphia, these activities were in full swing in 1993.

This is a story about an innovative partnership among community volunteers (park "friends" groups), a government agency (the Philadelphia Department of Recreation), and a nonprofit organization (the Pennsylvania Horticultural Society), which joined forces to reclaim and revitalize neighborhood parks in Philadelphia. It was an "arranged marriage" that faced considerable obstacles and challenges at the outset, and few were willing to bet on its success. Yet over the past fifteen years, through two different city mayors and new leadership at the government agency with each new administration, the arranged marriage not only met but also exceeded all expectations, goals, and benchmarks and found "love."

This story will explore the conditions that led to the partnership's creation, the strategies that allowed the relationship to grow and develop, and the lessons learned about what it takes to effect this level of change. It is a story of hope and sustainability. It sheds light on how organizations can form vital partnerships to achieve together what would be impossible to achieve separately.

The Conditions Are Set for an "Arranged Marriage"

A Distressed Situation for the Philadelphia Department of Recreation

Until recently, the parks in Philadelphia fell under the jurisdiction of two systems known as the Fairmount Park Commission (FPC) and the Philadelphia Department of Recreation (PDR). By 1993, due to years of budget cuts on the local, state, and federal levels, the parks in Philadelphia were in a state of crisis.

A large percentage of the neighborhood parks were in the domain of the Philadelphia Department of Recreation. Many of these parks had once been adequately staffed but were now in a constant state of *deferred maintenance*. This is "government speak" for acknowledging that everyone knows there is work that should be done, but that there is simply no money available to do it. This was a not a condition that PDR welcomed; it simply couldn't see a way to maintain the parks. The newly appointed commissioner was working hard to be strategic with the limited dollars in his budget. Staffed spaces such as recreation centers, pools, and ball fields received priority. Passive parks were at the bottom of the list.

The limited dollars allocated each year to the PDR budget meant, for example, that grass cutting occurred infrequently at best and without a regular schedule. Trash pickup was sporadic. As Joe Stephney, a PDR maintenance person, summed it up, "Frankly, if they didn't call us for an emergency situation, we rarely came to the parks." In fact, the commissioner, Michael DiBerardinis, was trying to interest the city in trading parks for the recreation centers and swimming pools that also existed in the Fairmount Park Commission. He argued, "Let's do what we do best and have the FPC do what they do best, and perhaps things would improve, and the community would be better served." However, for a variety of reasons the plan was not accepted, and the neighborhood parks—and by extension the neighborhoods—continued to suffer.

This situation left communities frustrated, overwhelmed, and angry. It left the PDR, frustrated, overwhelmed, and extremely defensive. The only time the PDR heard from the community was to complain or report a tragedy. As PDR employee Tom Fox described it, "We just drove our trucks en route to a center or pool or ball field and trained our eyes to look straight ahead. We didn't want to turn to the left or right to view the parks we had no resources to tend to."

An Opportunity for the Pennsylvania Horticultural Society

The Pennsylvania Horticultural Society (PHS), a nonprofit whose mission is to "improve the quality of life through horticulture," was about to receive an irresistible invitation to get involved in Philadelphia's park problem. The William Penn Foundation had just invested in the renovation of a senior citizens center called Center in the Park, located in Vernon Park in Germantown. The foundation had received a quick lesson in the many ways a neglected park becomes a liability for an entire community.

After the renovations were completed, foundation officials were appalled to realize that the seniors were afraid to come into the center through the front door. They did not feel safe in the park, which was not only unkempt but also dangerous. Not wanting to see its investment wasted, the foundation challenged PHS to improve the situation and offered the money to do so. The invitation was clear and direct: improve the park, build a partnership to do it, and develop a strategy to sustain the improvements.

Through its Philadelphia Green Program, PHS had a reputation for building successful partnerships to revitalize neglected spaces in the city. While new to the arena of neighborhood parks, the organization had worked closely with volunteer groups to create community gardens. PHS knew well the ancient wisdom that when people come together to work on the land, something powerful takes place. The work and the land have an ability to bring people together, to focus, to heal, and to transform not only the landscape but also the larger community.

And a Challenge

But what type of partnership would PHS need to create? It was relatively easy for PHS to work with others to make beautiful things grow in a specific, distressed environment. It's quite another thing to transform many locations and do it in a way that could build strong working relationships, generate new resources, create a system of maintenance, and last well into the future. If the Vernon Park project was successful, could it be replicated on a citywide scale? For improving one park was not the solution. Reforming an entire system was the larger vision and the answer to this irresistible invitation.

Perhaps like many partnerships arranged by an outsider, the partners moved forward not fully understanding the challenges or the opportunities. They learned quickly that what they focus on would be magnified, so they began simply and focused on Vernon Park. In time, the land, the people, and the relationships revealed extraordinary possibilities.

Results

It is now 2008, fifteen years later, and the partners in this arranged marriage have found love, ownership, and investment. Much has changed. The partnership has survived two administrations with two very different leaders. It has also survived staff turnover, budget cuts, and layoffs. The results at a glance include the following:

- City and state investment in capital improvements in PDR parks grew from $1.5 million in the ten years prior to the project's inception to $13.2 million between 1993 and 2006.
- Over one hundred parks from both the FPC and PDR system participated in the project.
- Friends groups in the PDR system have raised approximately $1.5 million, and volunteers have contributed over 518,766 hours of labor. The federal government now assigns a value of $19.51 per volunteer hour. This means that over the fifteen years at the current rate, the park system has received $10,121,125 worth of services.
- Treasured community spaces have been restored. Thousands of new trees have been planted.
- Neighborhood parks have in some cases become the springboards and catalysts for larger neighborhood and city revitalization efforts in residential and commercial areas. In other cases, they have served as complementary efforts to existing revitalization initiatives. The liability has become the asset.
- The parks have become centers for neighborhood life, the way the early architects and dreamers of urban parks intended. Mothers no longer warn their children to stay out of the park. Parks are once again places to play, relax, exercise, gather, organize, and celebrate. In 1993 there were no programs in the PDR parks. In 2008 there were close to 200 programs organized by community volunteers.

The neighborhood park system within the PDR inventory still faces considerable challenges. Lack of resources remains an issue, but there is a basic level of service provided. There is a system for stewardship that is maintained, and the advocacy movement in support of parks has never been better informed, engaged, and effective.

How Did This Happen?

What allowed this transformation to take place? The answer is one simple word—*partnership*. But the type of partnership required to influence and change a system this large was anything but simple. It was built slowly over time and required a great deal of careful nurturing.

In building this partnership, the organizations allowed themselves to not only *share* ideas, resources, and practices but were willing to *change* their practice and systems for getting things done if it advanced the larger mission of improving and sustaining the parks in Philadelphia. Gradually, each of the partner organizations became willing to have their work informed and influenced by the larger partnership. This is one of the hallmarks of the story. In this story, the partners did not simply contribute their time, talent, and resources to reach a common goal. Time was invested in new ways, talents were identified and allowed to blossom, new capacity was built, and resources were redirected and expanded over time. Eventually, as the land was transformed, the partners were transformed in the process, and a system for sustaining this new level of stewardship was put in place.

Lessons Learned

The following are personal insights that may be useful to others involved in cross-boundary collaborations.

An invitation that comes with resources is a big plus, perhaps a must.

While the initial grant to PHS was modest in size, it enabled PHS to bring money to the table with the government. Our undertaking was a bit of a high-stakes card game, and we would not have been taken very seriously if we did not have some resources to get into the game. A good idea was not enough in this situation.

On a long journey, patience and persistence are critical.

Even with the dollars, it wasn't enough to get the landowners (or those with responsibility for the parks) to reverse their practices. When dealing with an underresourced system with multiple demands, patience and persistence are essential. As the former PDR Commissioner DiBerardinis noted, "My initial impression was that they [PHS] were nice people who meant well but who didn't understand the complexity of the situation. I was sure they would go away sooner rather then later. I was not in any rush to get this new initiative on my radar screen, with all the other challenges." But PHS stayed committed and in time caught PDR's attention. "After many months, when my initial strategy of trading parks for pools failed to get traction, I began to think maybe, through this partnership, something that seemed impossible could become possible," said the commissioner. "We certainly couldn't do it alone."

"Low-hanging fruit" provides nourishment for the journey, and early success builds momentum.

Once the partnership was born, it was important that there be some early, concrete accomplishments to build confidence. In the world of park revitalization, this "low-hanging fruit" took the form of (1) ridding the park of trash, weeds, and debris; (2) mowing the grass; (3) planting an entrance garden; and (4) pruning trees. In addition, establishing weekly two-hour volunteer workdays in spring, summer, and fall had minimal cost and made a significant difference when supported with a larger strategy.

Leadership support is critical when attempting to change entrenched systems. But don't rely solely on the leader. Build relationships broad *and* deep.

In this partnership, we were fortunate to secure the support of the PDR commissioner. Once he saw the value of this partnership and its capacity to leverage resources, he became its staunchest supporter. He used his leadership position to either inspire or require cooperation from various levels of PDR. But we knew that while the leader had to sanction the work, it would be the hands-on staff members who would implement the new way of doing things. We wanted to maximize the buy-in and investment with this sector of the partnership.

To that end, PHS facilitated monthly operations team meetings. The purpose of this forum was to allow key staff from both PHS and PDR to meet and focus on the day-to-day work in parks. We came together to plan, solve problems, and evaluate the outcomes. The meetings offered an opportunity to ensure that the park agenda was not lost in the midst of issues related to recreation centers, pools, ball fields, and a host of political requests. In setting up this meeting, it was critical to be sure we had the right people at the table from the government. We needed people who understood the work and its challenges, and to maximize the effectiveness of this forum, we needed people with the authority to make decisions. Fifteen years later, this forum remains a critical component to the success of the partnership.

A small thing is a big thing.

The case of the park benches provides a wonderful illustration of the need to have the right people at the table. When we first began to revitalize neighborhood parks, the community groups requested that we remove broken benches. The benches in neglected parks were part of the problem. At best they were nonfunctional eyesores that detracted from the aesthetics of the park. At worst they provided places for drug sales, substance abuse, and prostitution. Many friends groups in the early years had a similar refrain: "Take out the benches!" and PDR obliged.

As the parks were reclaimed and revitalized, a new refrain was sung: "Bring the benches back!" Once a symbol of neglect and abuse, benches were now harbingers of the improving health and vitality of the parks. Mothers were returning with their children and wanted a place to sit and watch them on the swings. Seniors wanted a place to rest and converse. People of all ages wanted to sit and enjoy the clean, green, and safe oases of their neighborhood parks. But we couldn't seem to get the benches back.

For two years we made plans that were never carried out. No one seemed to understand the source of the delay. One day we finally asked the obvious, "Do we have the right people at the table to solve this problem? Why don't we get one of the bench makers to come to the meeting and help us find the solution?"

Within minutes of his appearance at the next meeting, John Kalasunas, a carpenter with the PDR, (who like his coworkers has many other tasks at the department), had the problem identified and solved. It turned out that bench requests were coming in the spring. This is one of the busiest months for the skilled tradespeople, who are preparing for pool season at that time. The bench orders were being put aside and lost in the process.

John suggested we submit the requests in the early winter. He also noted a problem with only having one mold to make the concrete portion of the benches and the need for additional training to assist with the masonry. Now, you could be reading this and wondering why this had not been communicated earlier. But if you work in government, you know that under the pressure of doing more and more with less, such conversations often don't occur.

The carpenter was glad to be part of the solution and felt valued and appreciated. His solution made sense, and the partnership was able to leverage the resources to get the additional molds, provide the additional training, and change the time frame for bench requests. The first benches built using this process were not only done on time; they also had a new artistic component. The carpenters, on their own initiative, carved into the back of each bench:

Philadelphia Department of Recreation, Philadelphia Green, Community Partnerships for Parks

The higher level of craftsmanship was living proof of the power of this unique partnership. The benches became a symbol not only of the health of the parks but also of the vitality of the partnership.

In a partnership that seeks to change systems, your problems are my problems.

How many times in the course of collaboration do we find ourselves thinking, *That's just not my problem. I'm delivering on my end. They have to do the same.* While we started with the same attitude, our thinking soon changed.

The monthly operations meeting became a place to share each other's work systems, priorities, and challenges. In the process, we began to *care about each other's problems.* We offered suggestions, options, and resources to one another. In time trust was built, accountability and follow-through improved, and the work became rewarding. As Tyronne Foster, a member of the maintenance division, described it, "Of all the work I have done for the PDR, the neighborhood park work means the most. I feel like we are not just picking up trash anymore—a job that is in and of itself unrewarding—we are making a difference. There are lots of people to help from the community and Philadelphia Green. My crew can get twice as much done in half the time because of this partnership."

This forum has been meeting on the third Wednesday of each month at lunchtime for the past ten years. The commissioner has changed as have key personnel in the maintenance division and in Philadelphia Green. But the commitment of those involved has remained strong. "These meetings are essential," says Barbara McCabe, parks coordinator for the PDR. "It's where we put our heads together and make sense of problems that a few years ago would have seemed insurmountable. Each partner has something unique to bring to the table, which really helps. And the lunch is also a big plus."

In addition to the monthly operations meeting, a bimonthly steering committee meets in the evening and provides a forum for community volunteers, government, Philadelphia Green, the Philadelphia Parks Alliance (a local advocacy coalition), and other key stakeholders to plan, problem solve, share resources, evaluate, and build the larger park advocacy movement. "This is the place where community, government, Philadelphia Green, and our advocacy group, the Philadelphia Parks Alliance can all work through challenges, come up with new and creative solutions, and be a great source of support to each other," says John Boyce, president of the Friends of Gorgas Park. "I can sometimes arrive tired from work but leave excited to do something great for my park, my neighborhood, and the city I love."

Use setbacks as springboards for growth and change.

Ensuring that community residents had ample opportunity to get involved with their parks was very important. It was the third leg of the partnership stool. The ability of Philadelphia Green to come to the community not as an expert but as a partner was key. It was important to spend time in the community to learn what was important to the residents about their parks. What was their vision? What were their concerns? What role could they play in the stewardship equation?

Early on we established a "partner park" program. Three parks were selected for this honor. It meant that each of the parks would receive about $60,000 to be used toward its revitalization over the course of three years. In return, each partner park had to agree to work on three things: growing their volunteer stewardship group, developing their capacity to secure additional resources, and bringing the community to their park and their park to the larger community.

In Philadelphia Green's eagerness to be clear and efficient, a staff member created a partner park agreement. The intention was to clarify each partner's responsibilities. The impact, however, was quite different with at least one of the key groups. They found the agreement off-putting. It was reminiscent of prior negative experiences of outsiders—usually of a different skin color—who came in to their community to tell them how to do things. It wasn't the result of listening and collaborating. It felt one-sided and was not acceptable.

When Philadelphia Green learned of the group's reaction, we had to work through a fair amount of defensiveness. We knew our intentions were good, and it was much more comfortable to be accountable for our good intentions and not be accountable for the impact of our actions. In time the staff came to see that it would have been better to meet together with the leadership of the interested groups and develop the agreement together. As an organization that also prides itself on "failing forward"—having the ability learn from our mistakes—we took steps to correct the situation. We accepted responsibility for the misunderstanding, apologized, and worked in partnership with the community to jointly develop a new partnership agreement.

The new agreement was not very much different from the first one, but the process was radically different. The right people were at the table to create it. We learned about each other's obligations and challenges. There was real give and take, and that made all the difference.

Owning our mistake and being ready to proceed in a different way was huge for the partnership. It's not unlike a personal relationship when you have your first fight. If you learn to navigate that together successfully with respect, honesty, and a spirit of compromise, you have created an important foundation for future work. The trust that was developed in those early days has served us well as we continue to navigate the turbulent water of conflict and missteps. As community leader Doris Gwaltney reflected, "That's when I knew this was different. The ability to say you are sorry and be willing to do something about it was big. We hadn't experienced that before, and we knew something special was going to happen for our park and the Carroll Park community."

Ordinary acts of kindness yield extraordinary results.

I have stated that initiating a partnership is easier when you can bring resources to the table, but this next lesson shows that some very valuable things have nothing to do with money.

When the partnership began, government and community were highly suspicious of each other. The only time government heard from the community was when they needed to express their frustration and complaints. The only time community saw government in their neighborhood parks was when they created a significant storm to get its attention. Changing this paradigm was critical.

Once government and community began to work together, relationships were formed. Individuals were no longer anonymous voices at the other end of the phone. When government found ways to provide basic levels of service to parks, the residents appreciated it and called to express that appreciation.

"I'll never forget the day when Facetta Green [the administrative assistant] picked up the phone prepared for another set of angry calls and said 'Listen everybody, someone is calling to say thanks,'" recalled PDR staff member Joe Stephney.

Throughout the past fifteen years, we have found multiple ways to say thanks. Examples include the following:

- An annual recognition event that thanks all of the community volunteers
- An Above and Beyond the Call award presented annually to an employee of PDR who has provided special service to the parks and community groups
- An annual field trip for park employees to learn about best practices in other park districts and share their own
- A plumbers and electricians' lunch to share the accomplishments of the prior year and plan for the season ahead.

A successful partnership requires attention to both product and process.

In this story, PHS has played an important "process" role. While all staff involved understand the importance of not only *what* we do but *how* we do it, a few people must play an active role in this aspect of the work. A complex partnership needs a person with the skills to facilitate a collaborative relationship. A person from one of the partner organizations must have his or her eyes, heart, hands, and mind on this aspect of the work to ensure it doesn't get lost in the sea of demands, time frames, and challenges. Process must be understood as *essential* to the success of the partnership. In many partnerships, the process and relationships receive little attention until the partners hit a wall and need to hire a consultant to get them past it.

In this partnership—because we are working on a large scale and building relationships broad and deep—the job of tending to the relationship must be expanded to more than one person. This requires that the lead person build the capacity of other staff to tend to the relationships at varying levels. Staff must be equipped to facilitate effective meetings, learn how to navigate conflict and compromise, communicate effectively, engage in active listening, and learn the art of meeting people more than halfway while building accountability and investment.

We came together to clean up a neglected public space. We wanted to transform an abandoned landscape and we all became transformed in the process.

—*Joan Reilly*

Sustained transformation of land requires transformation of people.

Our initial invitation was to transform a park. It didn't take long to realize that the improvement of one park was important, but the improvement of all parks was really the opportunity and the nobler goal. To change the park system on a citywide scale, more resources needed to be leveraged, and a larger circle of stakeholders had to be formed. This would require strategic thinking informed by the experiences of other cities and park systems. But none of this would have been possible on such a large scale if the people, the primary core of the three partnership entities, were not willing to enter into the process of growth and change. No one entity could serve as the expert. All needed be learners on this journey.

The PDR had ultimate responsibility and authority for the parkland, yet their openness to new ways of working was astonishing. The community, despite years of neglect and disappointment, was open to moving from a position of adversary to full-fledged partner who not only helped identify problems but became an integral part of the solution. Philadelphia Green moved from "expert" to learner in a way that facilitated the journey for each and all. Each partner changed in similar and different ways, and the fruits of the collective labor are visible each day in our neighborhood parks and in the communities and city they serve.

Joan Reilly is a senior director at the Pennsylvania Horticultural Society, overseeing its nationally recognized urban greening program, Philadelphia Green. She can be reached at *jreilly@pennhort.org.*

IV. CULTIVATING NEW RESOURCES

Patrick Sanaghan and Susan Felker

Challenge: How a new leader used a collaborative planning process to educate himself and create a shared vision for a large state department

Introduction

THE PENNSYLVANIA DEPARTMENT of Conservation and Natural Resources (DCNR) is a complex, midsize state agency with a budget of approximately $400 million. It has about 1,400 salaried and 1,900 wage-earning employees, most of whom work in state park and forest field offices throughout the state.

DCNR manages 117 state parks and 2.1 million acres of state forestland. Its charge also includes providing information on the state's ecological and geological resources and managing a variety of grant and technical assistance programs addressing community recreation, heritage areas, rivers conservation, greenways and trails, and natural areas and open space.

Michael DiBerardinis became secretary of DCNR in 2003. He came to DCNR with extensive experience with large urban government and foundations. He was also well versed in collaborative leadership and management practices.

With the help of an outside consultant he had worked with previously as well as his executive team, DiBerardinis created an extensive collaborative statewide planning process involving more than 1,800 people throughout the state. His goal was to build a powerful future for DCNR through engagement, listening, reflection, and leadership. Through a yearlong planning process, he developed an action plan that would guide the agency's direction and resources over the next several years.

Says Secretary DiBerardinis, "I knew from the very beginning that I had to engage staff and stakeholders as I came on board. There was so much to learn about the complexity of a state agency. So I went out and talked with people, listened, and reflected on what I was learning. I've found that by doing this, everybody's thinking is changed and advanced as a result and that real relationships are built by the transparent process.

"In my first six months, I met with hundreds of people in what felt like hundreds of meetings. It was the best way for me to make sense of the issues I had inherited and the complexities I was going to face."

Creating the Action Plan

The secretary began by identifying several important guiding principles that would help govern the planning process and hold the department accountable to internal and external stakeholders. They were as follows:

1. Transparent Communication

The department had to be committed to communicating effectively with internal and external stakeholders. This was not meant to be a secretive process where a few people knew what was going on. DiBerardinis wanted everyone to feel informed throughout the process. This was done in several ways:

- Planning updates were shared at weekly executive team meetings, monthly external advisory council meetings, and specific meetings with external stakeholders.
- An internal travel blog detailed the secretary's travels throughout the state and what he was learning from his interaction with employees.
- Web pages, easily accessible to internal and external stakeholders, kept people informed about the overall planning process.
- After every interactive planning meeting, an informal report of the results was either sent to participants directly or posted on the Web page for review.

2. Meaningful Engagement of Stakeholders

All of the internal and external stakeholder meetings were designed for maximum participation and interaction. Trained internal facilitators were used to manage the meetings so that they produced real outcomes and allowed for maximum conversation and interaction. Small groups shared ideas, synthesized information, and produced recommendations.

DiBerardinis listened to stakeholders carefully and allowed their contributions to influence the planning process (e.g., white papers). DCNR created the opportunity for diverse groups (both internal and external) to talk with each other about the issues and share their different ideas and perspectives. Respectful discussion and dialogue were encouraged.

Says the secretary, "True collaboration has to be organized and disciplined. It just doesn't happen by itself. When you work with large groups, you have to intentionally design the interaction to ensure that all voices are heard. It's a very thoughtful process."

3. DCNR Had to "Own" the Process

Although the secretary used the services of a trusted and experienced external consultant, he did not want an "expert" telling him what the department should do. The consultant was charged with designing the collaborative planning process with him, but DCNR employees would do most of the thinking and working. The secretary wanted DCNR employees to be both authors and owners of the planning process. Steps that were taken included the following:

- Well-trained internal staff facilitated dozens of meetings across the state.
- The internal staff wrote, edited, and revised the concept papers and synthesized them into the final action plan.
- The secretary or members of his executive team presided at every meeting to show the importance the senior leadership team placed on the process.
- A core planning team, along with the secretary's executive team, established the guiding principles for the process and held everyone accountable for adherence to them.
- The role of the planning consultant was to facilitate meetings, not deliver key messages or summarize information. This was done by senior DCNR leaders.

The Collaborative Journey

The yearlong planning process had five distinct phases:

1. Data gathering and engagement
2. Getting organized operationally
3. Sensemaking and feedback

4. Vision conferences
5. Action plan

1. The "Road Show": Data Gathering and Engagement

The secretary began his tenure with an extended series of interactive meetings with both internal and external stakeholders throughout the state. The purposes of these meetings were

- to meet and greet people throughout the state and begin to build relationships,
- to engage their thinking about the future hopes and challenges of DCNR, and
- to *listen* to and *learn* from the interaction and discussions.

These early meetings were used to gather strategic information. Each group was asked to answer directed focus questions that provided useful information. Here are some examples:

- What does DCNR do well?
- How can DCNR improve its services?
- What challenges and opportunities do you see DCNR facing in the next few years? (What are the opportunities for growth and advancement?)
- What advice do you have for the secretary?

Early messages indicated that the agency had established a strong foundation since its creation in 1995 and that the opportunity now existed for the agency to expand its mission to be a leading advocate and steward for the natural resources of the state. As Secretary DiBerardinis later wrote,

> As my touring continued throughout the state, a message that was communicated over and over again by external stakeholders was *think regionally*. People were telling us that we were doing a good job with our individual programs but that we needed to look at what we did in a broader and larger context.

This meant that as a department we had to apply our resources, investments and thinking in a coherent and strategic way within a specific regional context. It has greatly influenced our practice on the ground.

More than eight hundred surveys were collected during this phase of the planning process, including about 42 percent from external stakeholders and 58 percent from internal staff. The majority, 82 percent, were paper surveys collected at meetings, with another 18 percent completed online.

Several important themes emerged from the survey data. These became the "conceptual buckets" that would later form the strategic planning themes for the entire process.

The nine themes were the following:

- Management of DCNR lands
- Environmental education and stewardship
- Economic development through tourism and forest products
- Land conservation
- Outdoor recreation
- Counties, cities, and towns
- Private forestlands stewardship
- Conservation science and biodiversity
- Greenways and trails

Editor's Note: *During most senior leadership transitions, the usual way a new leader "learns" about the organization is through briefing books, reports, climate surveys, targeted interviews with key individuals, and possibly small focus groups. Secretary DiBerardinis did all these traditional things, but it was not enough for him. He needed to engage people face-to-face. This kind of approach, when done well and authentically, does several important things:*

1. *It communicates to stakeholders that the new leader respects others' opinions and is willing to listen.*
2. *It more fully informs the leader about the complexity, culture, strengths, and challenges of the organization (things you never really learn by reading briefing books).*
3. *It creates a sense of energy and positive momentum because ideas are being exchanged and relationships are being built during the engagement process.*
4. *It sets a leadership tone that promotes engagement and collaboration, not for a one-shot deal but for carrying out all business in the future.*

2. Getting Organized (Creating the Internal Mechanism to Support the Planning Process)

Concurrent with the secretary's travels, internal mechanisms were developed to guide and support the work ahead. Communicating the high priority he placed on the planning process, the secretary appointed a special assistant to head the initiative and manage the process and the various leadership and work teams. Each team had unique roles and responsibilities.

The Core Planning Team

The five-person core planning team included top- and midlevel policy, communication, and outreach experts. Their role was to do the "big thinking" about the planning process (e.g., Who do we need to engage? What is a realistic timeline? What are the key components of our internal and external communication strategy?).

This team was also responsible for reviewing and editing written products as well as integrating all the complex parts of the planning process. The secretary met with this team on a regular basis.

The Resource and Implementation Team (RIT)

This twelve-member team included the core team members and representative senior staff. This team was given decision-making authority, and their meetings were focused and outcome driven. They acted as a sounding board; advisors and troubleshooters; recruiters of and coaches for writing team leaders; reviewers of concept papers; and reporters keeping the secretary informed about challenges, problems, and progress.

The Writing Teams

The writing teams consisted of content experts in each of the nine conceptual buckets identified during the phase 1 data gathering and engagement. The RIT nominated co-leaders for each writing team, and the secretary confirmed these nominations. The secretary then met with the writing team leaders to give them their charge, answer their questions, and share his thinking about the emerging themes. The co-leaders created their own teams to write their particular white paper, and the teams were vetted and approved by the RIT.

Using Internal Talent: Other Informal Teams

DCNR is a complex, multiple-office statewide organization. It utilized internal technology and communication expertise to ensure regular dissemination of quality information and created user-friendly mechanisms for feedback and discussion.

E-mail communication became an important component of the communication and engagement process, and e-mail distribution lists were created for all team members to keep everyone informed and connected, with interaction and cross-dialogue encouraged. Internal Web designers regularly updated internal/external Web content for employees and the general public to keep them apprised of the progress. DCNR used internal IT experts to recommend methods and mechanisms for analyzing the eight hundred-plus surveys, develop an interactive database, and generate reports for the writing teams.

Editor's Note: *Collaborative planning is not an informal process but has real structure and discipline built in. Its minimal but well-designed structure allows for engagement, dialogue, synthesis, and, most importantly, learning. The different teams that were put together, the communication protocols that were established, and the guiding principles adhered to all created the space for collaborative work to take place.*

3. Sensemaking and Feedback

Discussion Briefs

After much discussion and dialogue, it was agreed that the nine conceptual buckets would provide the framework for written discussion briefs, which would help create realistic boundaries about the scope of the planning process and provide it with appropriate focus. The secretary charged the writing teams to draft these discussion briefs, which were to be layperson friendly and highly informative. The goal was to produce something an average citizen could read and understand in about twenty to thirty minutes.

Each discussion brief was limited to about five pages and included (1) a description of the issue with historical context and pertinent background information; (2) the identification of challenges and issues regarding the specific theme; and (3) an articulation of future possibilities, alternatives, and options. Writing teams were very careful to write these papers in neutral terms and not show any internal biases.

The secretary wanted to ensure that the discussion briefs were honest, informative, and on-target. He directed internal staff to hold a series of validation meetings to seek dialogue and feedback about the briefs from internal and external stakeholders. A series of facilitated meetings (one per discussion brief) were held with close to two hundred participants. About 70 percent of participants were external stakeholders, representing some ninety-seven organizations.

Writing team leaders participated in their paper's validation meeting to provide explanation as necessary and to hear feedback firsthand. The writing team leaders left each meeting with all the feedback data on flip charts. They used this information to work with their teams to produce a second draft or white paper.

White Papers

The white papers were organized according to a set structure and were of limited length. The white papers were delivered back to the validation meeting attendees for comments. The final drafts were reviewed by the resource and implementation team and the secretary and posted on the internal and external Web sites with an invitation to give feedback. The white papers were used in the vision conferences to inform participants and ground the discussions with accurate information.

Editor's Note: *It is unusual to have this kind of double-loop feedback process with discussion briefs. Most of the time, these briefs are written internally to inform the vision process. The secretary took the additional step in creating the opportunity for external feedback and validation. He wanted to ensure that the discussion briefs had integrity and that all stakeholders trusted the data.*

4. *The Vision Conferences (Creating a Shared Picture)*

The external planning consultant worked with the secretary and members of the core planning team to design three vision conferences across the state (Pittsburgh, State College, and Allentown), including internal and external stakeholders. About fifty participants attended each conference with about a 60 percent external, 40 percent internal mix.

Each conference was a full day in length and was designed for maximum participation and interaction. Using the white papers, participants created shared pictures of the future for each of the nine strategic themes. Participants were also asked to think deeply *across* all nine themes and identify potential points of leverage, integration, and partnership. The secretary participated in each planning conference, and members of the secretary's executive team and bureau directors attended at least one conference.

5. Action Plan

The products of the three planning conferences informed the leaders of the action plan writing team. The team met and reviewed the planning conference flip charts and identified key messages and driving themes. The core planning team developed an outline for the action plan, members of the resource and implementation team and writing teams reviewed it, and the core team then wrote a draft plan with the press secretary as lead writer.

A draft action plan was produced within two months of the vision conferences. The secretary approved the draft, and it was posted on the intranet for employees to review and offer feedback, anonymously if they chose.

Internal Validation and Ownership of the Action Plan

Once the draft action plan was written, a series of six regional and two central office meetings were held for DCNR staff over a two-week period. These meetings were designed to engage employee thinking about the proposed plan, seek their feedback, and discuss implications for their work. The secretary fully realized that staff ownership was essential to the plan's success. He wanted their agreement that this plan was worthy of their commitment and effort over the next five years. Approximately 250 staff attended these meetings.

The secretary opened and closed the first of these staff meetings, which was facilitated by the planning consultant. Subsequent meetings were facilitated by internal facilitators and opened/closed by senior staff.

External Validation

DCNR also conducted an interactive external stakeholder meeting to invite feedback and review by outside partners. This feedback informed the final version of the action plan.

Outcomes of the Action Plan Process

1. A program called TreeVitalize has been created to help plant thousands of trees in urban neighborhoods across the state. Service foresters are helping urban residents plant trees in their neighborhoods. Other partners (e.g., Eagles football organization) have contributed money and resources.

2. DCNR is leading seven conservation landscape initiatives (CLIs) throughout the state. The purpose of these CLIs is to engage nonprofits, foundations, and local governments to work together to protect and preserve the unique natural resources in their geographic areas. This is one of the largest cross-boundary, geographically diverse collaborations in the country.

3. DCNR leads a *land protection initiative* that works with leaders of land conservancies and foundations across the state to help protect land throughout Pennsylvania. This is the first time these diverse groups of influential stakeholders have worked together to think about a coherent statewide approach to land protection.

4. An internal survey of all DCNR employees conducted by the Human Resources Bureau showed that over 80 percent of employees felt "engaged to very engaged" about the work of the department. They reported renewed enthusiasm for the mission and vision of DCNR and excitement about the future.

5. The secretary created an internal, statewide *leadership development program (LDP)*, which has involved almost two hundred leaders and managers throughout the department. This program focuses on collaborative leadership practices, models, and theories and teaches each participant about facilitation and meeting design. These leaders are expected to engage stakeholders throughout the state in ongoing assessment and feedback.

When collaborative practices are principled, it can elevate your chances for success. You don't collaborate to make it look like you are listening or engaging people. It must have transparency and integrity. People need to believe that their ideas and participation really matter, that they make a difference by being part of the process.
—Secretary Michael DiBerardinis

Lessons Learned

1. Collaboration is hard work!

Creating a collaborative planning process that meaningfully engages hundreds of stakeholders isn't easy! It takes an enormous amount of time, thinking, discussion, and planning. DCNR assigned its best people to the process, and it was still a difficult journey. However, the process generated much enthusiasm among both internal staff and external stakeholders, and DCNR is pleased and proud of the product.

2. Leadership visibility is essential.

Collaborative planning cannot be delegated to some internal planning group. The secretary owned the process by being at the planning meetings, defining his purposes and goals, attending many of the discussion brief and white paper meetings, and attending all of the visioning conferences. His presence communicated the importance he placed on the process and showed his interest, commitment, and ownership.

3. Utilize and build the capacity of employees.

DCNR would not have been able to pull off this large and complicated process without a great deal of help from internal staff. Staff participated in the following ways:

- Writing teams crafted the discussion briefs and white papers.
- Internal facilitators conducted scores of meetings throughout the state.
- Members of the core team and staff managed the logistical challenges of scheduling meeting rooms, communicating schedules, reaching out to external stakeholders, and recruiting and providing additional training to facilitators.
- DCNR technology staff developed the database and managed the internal and external Web pages.
- Internal communications and technology staff developed messages, did substantial writing and editing, maintained Web information, and managed e-mail lists.

By using internal staff, DCNR was able to save hundreds of thousands of dollars and, at the same time, build the strategic skill set of its employees. The department now more deeply understands how qualified and dedicated its staff really is.

4. Communicate, Communicate, Communicate!

DCNR made great efforts to keep people informed throughout the process. This included scores of face-to-face meetings using a *variety* of communication vehicles. The goal was to employ a combination of high tech and "high touch" communication.

- The core team and resource and implementation team met constantly to review purposes and collaborate and coordinate their efforts. After "road show" meetings, the secretary often sent an e-mail message to internal staff, directing them to his blog, where he recapped whom he met with and what he learned. (People liked this a lot.)
- White papers and the draft plan were posted so people could offer feedback. E-mail messages from the secretary kept employees and external participants updated throughout the planning process.
- DCNR replied to e-mail comments and, at a minimum, said thank you. Specific issues were often addressed directly.

5. Collaboration Builds Trust.

When your process is transparent and people can see that their participation influences and guides decision making, it builds trust, and with trust, many things are possible. DCNR cannot achieve all it wants to accomplish in the action plan all by itself. It needs the work, action, and thinking of others. Partners are emerging; other organizations are beginning to take real leadership around CLIs and land protection, and voters are supporting these efforts. For the most part, internal and external stakeholders trust the department's intentions and ability to deliver on promises and are committed to ongoing collaboration in the future.

Patrick Sanaghan is president of the Sanaghan Group (*sanaghan@aol. com*). Susan Felker is director of DCNR's Office of Policy and Planning. (*sfelker@state.pa.us*)

V. THE ROAD TO COLLABORATION

Amy Steffen and Lonnie Weiss

Challenge: How to create dialogue between parties who are in tense disagreement and develop a constructive process for moving forward

Introduction

T HE TRAFFIC WAS a nightmare. During rush hour, it could take forty-five minutes to drive a one-mile stretch of road punctuated by three traffic lights. Side streets were jammed with commuters seeking shortcuts, and local residents struggled to pull out of their driveways during the rush. The house-rattling din of constant traffic undermined the quality of life for residents. This was the situation on and around U.S. Route 1, the primary north-south artery in the Penns Neck area of central New Jersey, near Princeton.

These conditions had been worsening since the mid-1980s, despite attention from the New Jersey Department of Transportation (NJDOT). Traffic volume far exceeded road capacity in four municipalities in the Princeton area. Residents proclaimed their frustration to elected officials at township meetings while the local paper, *The Princeton Packet*, ran editorials and letters bewailing the situation. Resolving the traffic was high priority for all four mayors, and they were active participants in a regional transportation forum.

Despite this urgency, an acceptable solution was elusive. A complex intersection of players and concerns was entangled, just as the traffic along Route 1 was jammed. The most recent proposal by NJDOT, the result of fifteen years of planning and negotiating, was met with approval by some and outrage by others. The plan to build a new two-lane county road near the Millstone River, thus bypassing the traffic lights and congestion on Route 1, became known as the Millstone Bypass. Some homeowners, eager for relief from the congestion that plagued their small streets, embraced the plan. Others complained that the proposal was unfair and would dump even more traffic on to their streets. Watershed advocates protested it, decrying the ruination of a clean and quiet stretch of river. A multitude of stakeholders joined the controversy, some pushing for quick relief to the traffic congestion and others advocating for protection of environmental and cultural sites. It seemed that these two basic goals—traffic relief and protection of resources—were irreconcilably at odds.

The proposed Millstone Bypass engendered so much controversy that then-Governor Christine Whitman was brought into the fray. She took the unprecedented move of intervening in the affairs of the NJDOT, ordering them to halt their plans and conduct an environmental impact statement (EIS) on the proposed roadway. This meant the NJDOT was effectively back at square one. An EIS entails considering all reasonable alternatives to a proposed action, evaluating their environmental impacts, and selecting a preferred alternative. The preferred alternative must balance the benefits of an action with the mandate to avoid, mitigate, or remediate any adverse environmental impacts. The process also requires public participation. Would a new study resolve the controversy? What if lots of time and money were spent to find a new solution and it too was met with protest and lawsuits?

An Opportunity to Collaborate

Faced with a highly polarized and conflicted situation, NJDOT Commissioner James Weinstein decided to overhaul the process for finding a solution. In the spring of 2001, the commissioner announced a radically new approach to solving the Penns Neck congestion problem. "The NJDOT is committed to taking an entirely fresh look at this project," he said. "Everything is on the table, and we intend to proceed by bringing everyone who has a stake in this project's future to the table." In short, the commissioner had put collaboration at the *center* of the process.

The NJDOT would complete an environmental impact statement and far exceed the standard level of public involvement. The full array of stakeholder groups would be invited to participate in an in-depth problem-solving forum called the Partners' Roundtable. The commissioner believed that by getting everyone in the same room and giving everyone a role in finding a solution, they could change the dynamic of conflict and find consensus. The structure of the Partners' Roundtable created new roles for the DOT and the citizen stakeholders. The NJDOT was no longer at the hub, mediating the various conflicts and concerns. Stakeholders were consulted at every step of the way and had responsibility for agreeing to a solution. It was a degree of collaboration never before attempted by the department. It would be a significant innovation of the public-involvement process linked to an EIS.

Eventually, this great experiment in collaboration did succeed. The seemingly intractable conflict that had stalled progress on U.S. Route 1 for nearly twenty years came to a sound conclusion that was both technically astute and supported by the people who had to live with it. Moreover, the solution balanced the need to relieve traffic congestion while preserving environmental resources. This chapter highlights key elements of the collaboration's success.

New Leadership and a New Project Team

For the study to operate effectively, it needed new leadership. During the Millstone Bypass controversy, the DOT had become an object of distrust, the engineering consultants were roundly disliked, and the data were questioned. A new project team was formed and was charged with bringing together very disparate stakeholders and making room for collaboration. The project team had to be perceived as unbiased and trustworthy.

Understanding this situation, the commissioner went outside the normal NJDOT leadership circle. He installed leaders of the Voorhees Transportation Policy Center of Rutgers University at the helm. Martin Robins, then director of the center, had over thirty years of experience as a transportation planner and was known and respected by the people within NJDOT. Assistant Director Jon Carnegie was an innovative transportation planner who was knowledgeable about the interplay of transportation, land use, and the environment. As policy people, both Martin and Jon were interested in improving the decision-making process and had no stake in the specific outcome. As a DOT manager put it, "We hired Rutgers because we wanted an unbiased third party that was free of past prejudices."

Inside the DOT, different staff members were assigned to the project. The lead DOT roles went to members of the Environmental Division. Engineers were members of the team and contributed their technical expertise, but they did not choose the solutions and did not lead the team. Shifting leadership represented a huge departure for the department, signaling that environmental concerns were important and demonstrating a new openness to collaboration.

The project team included traffic engineers, environmental engineers, historic preservation process experts, public outreach experts, and a meeting facilitation team (the authors of this article). The technical consultants would collect data and analyze it, but they would stop short of drawing conclusions. The final meaning of the information would be determined in partnership with the roundtable. With new leadership, new staff, and strong group-process expertise, the project team was well positioned to engage and collaborate with the Partners' Roundtable.

The Use of a Partners' Roundtable

The Partners' Roundtable itself was a diverse and highly opinionated group of thirty-two stakeholders. In addition to the mayors of four municipalities and representatives from several state agencies, individuals representing a broad array of interests were included. Chambers of Commerce, the Sierra Club, Princeton University, neighborhood associations, a watershed association, and the corporate owner of the land on which the Millstone Bypass would have been built all participated. Every effort was made to be inclusive throughout the process. The roundtable worked in partnership with the project team. Stakeholders were now on the inside, working together.

The Partners' Roundtable was radically different from any previous DOT public engagement forum. Typically, when the DOT begins an EIS study, a project team is assembled to define the problem, generate alternative solutions, run traffic models to evaluate them, conduct environmental and other impact studies, analyze the data, and eventually recommend a preferred alternative.

Along the way, they inform the public and accept public input. Public participation is mandated, but participation is usually limited to input and reactions to drafts. For instance, in a typical public scoping forum, a panel of professionals led by DOT engineers presents the situation and project objectives. Citizens are allowed five minutes each to raise concerns and suggest alternatives. Timekeeping is rigorous, and a court stenographer records the proceedings. The DOT is the hub of all the proceedings, and they, not the public, are responsible for reconciling disparate views. This structure makes it nearly impossible to collaborate; there is simply no opportunity for give and take. In fact, meetings structured like this can encourage polarization as individuals advocate strongly, hoping their views will prevail.

In contrast, the Partners' Roundtable was designed to be an intimate and integral part of the entire process. The roundtable was established as an advisory committee of community partners from the public, private, and nonprofit sectors. The partners were asked to work together to consider the mobility issues in the area, address differences of opinion and approach, and strive for consensus on workable solutions. They essentially functioned as an extension of the project team, contributing to the final recommendation that went to the decision makers, the state DOT, and the Federal Highway Administration (FHWA).

This was a radically new role for the public and a risk for the DOT. Ideally, everyone would benefit from a consensus. The more agreement the community could reach, the more likely their preferences would be adopted by the decision makers. Yet support was not assured. Different factions were deeply suspicious of each other. Would the environmentalists benefit by stalling the process? Would leaders give special privileges to traditional power holders? When the Partners' Roundtable was announced, one advocacy group newsletter ran the headline "Real Opening or NJDOT Charm Offensive?" Even within the DOT, many doubted the usefulness of the endeavor, believing the originally proposed bypass was the best technical solution. Support had to be developed step by step.

Cast a Wide Net: Include a Variety of Stakeholders

DOT's commissioner declared the intention to be inclusive, saying the agency would "bring everyone who has a stake in this project's future to the table." But how do you truly welcome and engage people who hold diverse and polarized perspectives? It's tempting to exclude strongly opinionated or seemingly angry groups, but this nearly guarantees that they will protest any solution that they are not part of creating.

Wisely, the project team cast a wide net and methodically included everyone who was willing to participate. The project team reached out to the public, thoughtfully considered membership in the Partners' Roundtable, and opened all roundtable meetings to the public. Groups were invited to contribute in the following ways:

- *Public outreach.* One of the earliest efforts to engage people in open dialogue was a series of "listening sessions." Project team members conducted interviews with almost one hundred people representing forty-five local organizations. The team went to community settings and residents' living rooms to make it easy to participate. Their listening stance spoke volumes, demonstrating that this study would actively work with the public's concerns. This early outreach identified issues, opened the dialogue, and began to forge relationships and trust in the project team and the project.
- *Roundtable membership.* Identifying who would be named as official roundtable representatives was a sensitive decision. This effort had to

be visibly inclusive while retaining some efficiency in group size and process. Based on the early outreach and knowledge of active protesters and supporters of the Millstone Bypass, a group of diverse stakeholders was invited to participate on the roundtable. However, before finalizing the roundtable composition, the project leaders created a membership committee from this initial group of stakeholders.

The membership committee, not the project team, decided the logic and criteria for selecting roundtable representatives. At a hot moment much later, someone yelled at Jon Carnegie, "Who are you to decide who should be here!" He could honestly respond, "I didn't." Community members themselves had decided who to invite on to the roundtable.

- *Meeting participation.* Another critical decision was to open the Partners' Roundtable meetings to the public for participation as well as observation. No one was turned away, and a regular crowd began to attend. Common rules of engagement—one speaker at a time, with no interruption, wait to be called upon by the facilitator—were applied to all. Roundtable members sat at the table with name tents, and the general public sat in rows of chairs at the side of the room. Partners who wanted to speak stood their name tents on end; the general public simply raised their hand. It was clear that this was not a closed-door process.

As the DOT project leader saw it, at first "you could taste the skepticism." But over time people's trust grew in the process, in the project team, and even in their co-adversaries. Project leaders embraced broad engagement from the very start of the project, and they reaped the reward of a truly engaged community of stakeholders.

The Beginnings of Real Collaboration

An early task of the Partners' Roundtable was to establish goals and objectives for the project. This might have been done by DOT staff or the project team, with a perfunctory show of agreement from the public. In this case, however, a goals and objectives committee was established from among the roundtable members. The committee generated the goals and objectives and presented its recommendations to the whole roundtable for approval. The goal areas included transportation improvements, environmental protections, fair distribution of traffic on key streets, and protection of neighborhood integrity. Objectives under each goal added specificity. The list had power because it represented the real range of concerns in the community, and it came from the stakeholders themselves. Ultimately, these goals and objectives became the standards by which the group evaluated all the alternative road solutions at the end of the project.

The next project milestone was to define alternative solutions to the traffic congestion on U.S. Route 1 and the surrounding neighborhoods. The technical consultants presented the key elements of technically feasible solutions. Stakeholders combined them in various configurations over a course of three meetings. In total, the roundtable defined eighteen roadway alternatives, plus a no-build option. All parties had their say, and everyone saw that an option that addressed their initial desires was on the table. Again, the stakeholders, not the technical experts, were in the lead on defining their options.

Technical Studies

The heart of an environmental impact statement is a series of technical studies looking at roadway capacity; traffic volume; rush-hour delays; trip origins and destinations; demographic projections; documentation of historic, cultural, and natural resources; impacts on water and air quality; and more. The traffic benefits of each alternative solution and the no-build option are modeled to see how well each would perform. Then the environmental impacts of each solution are analyzed.

A rhythm of work emerged for the roundtable and the project team. Project staff and consultants conducted studies and documented the data and analysis. Staff distributed reports a week before the monthly roundtable meetings. At the meetings, they made presentations using large-scale maps and PowerPoint slides. Then they responded to questions from the diverse array of stakeholders.

These meetings could have been deadly boring or dangerously contentious. Instead, they hovered in the range of constructive and civil and sometimes verged into insightful and creative. Each roundtable meeting was a forum for collaboration enabled by strong leadership and meeting facilitation.

Transparency and Integrity of Data

The project team wanted a transparent process. They knew that in Penns Neck's atmosphere of low trust, any hint of "black box" secrecy would evoke crippling resistance. One guiding principle was that all information was shared with all. The public's suspicion of backroom deals strengthened the team's inclination to be transparent. They rigorously shared information, to the point of distributing all correspondence they received to the full roundtable.

The project team was committed to presenting data clearly and ensuring that people understood it. They took great pains to provide "Traffic 101" explanations, educating roundtable members on how they structured the data collection and analysis. They made sure the engineers' presentations could be grasped by laypeople and patiently explained concepts and specifics until they were clearly understood.

If roundtable members got stuck, the project team stopped to bring them along. As the DOT manager recalled, "We thought we had answered an issue ten meetings ago, but the team would go back if people had questions. In hindsight, some of these decisions were genius. At the time, it was driving me crazy. I was worried that people wanted to stop the process. But in slowing it down, we actually sped up."

Project leaders were firmly committed to finding the best outcome to the Penns Neck traffic congestion problems. They stayed unattached to any preconceived outcome and questioned assumptions. They pushed for precision on what the data really meant. Once, early analysis indicated that traffic congestion could only be reduced by solutions that included a controversial connector road. The project team pushed back and had the team study the data more carefully. They concluded that the difference in performance was minimal and kept all the potential solutions in play.

One roundtable member played a key role in the commitment to process integrity. This woman, a vocal critic who lived on one of the busy cross streets, approached the team early in the process. She told Martin Robins, "I believe you are a person of integrity. I feel I can trust you to produce a process that's credible and believable." Her confidence, entwined with a challenge, became a touchstone for Martin through the long complex process, bolstering his commitment to provide transparent and unassailable data.

The Role of Facilitation

In roundtable meetings, facilitation methods helped people understand the data and feel heard when they contributed. Recognizing that people cared deeply about their community and held good intentions, facilitators created a forum where people could risk acting collaboratively. Neutral facilitation and consistent meeting structure helped people trust the process. Facilitation methods included the following:

- Establishing rules that one person speaks at a time, speakers wait to be recognized, no one interrupts a speaker
- Reminding the group of their purpose and intentions
- Referencing the meeting's purpose when deciding whether to stick to the planned agenda or to digress;
- Structuring data presentation: twenty minutes of presentation, questions for clarification, another round of presentation and clarification, then discussion and
- Collecting several questions before responding to avoid the "tyranny of the first question" and allow experts to consider their responses.

Behind the scenes in project team meetings, facilitation helped translate technical data analysis into clearly communicated information. Facilitators provided a layperson's perspective and a reality check for the engineers. They gave advice on where to scale back content and "chunk" concepts bit by bit for nontechnical participants. Facilitators initiated regular project team conference calls for the day after each roundtable meeting to debrief, share impressions, and capture requests for data.

Time for a Decision

After nearly two years and more than thirty meetings, the technical analysis was largely complete. Now a decision had to be made. From among the nineteen roadway alternatives, one preferred alternative had to be chosen. The project team wrestled with how to proceed. Were they really going to ask all the partners in the roundtable to join them in a room to decide on a single solution?

The facilitator team proposed a series of interactive workshop-style meetings aimed at reaching consensus. They were confident that the group could be thoughtful and constructive in a carefully structured setting. Of course, no one knew what level of agreement was possible. It felt risky to try for agreement; a blowout at the end of the project would expose the solution to protest. On the other hand, consensus would bring closure to the roundtable and a clear path forward. Hedging their bets, the project team called the final sessions synthesis workshops rather than consensus meetings.

Planning the Synthesis Workshops

Planning the synthesis workshops was a challenge. Faced with the complexity of many partners, alternative solutions, and goals, the facilitator team convened a planning committee. The planning committee was a microcosm of the whole roundtable, representing the range of constituencies. Many members were outspoken and opinionated, making their participation very valuable. The planning committee's job was to determine specific goals for the synthesis workshops and to provide feedback on the meeting design. They also served as ambassadors to the other members, lending credibility to the synthesis endeavor.

At the first planning committee meeting, facilitators asked the group to imagine that the synthesis workshops had been a great success. Then they asked what had gone well and what had been accomplished. Two clear themes emerged. First, the partners wanted to understand each others' perspectives, to walk in each others' shoes. Second, they wanted to make sense of all that they had heard and draw their own conclusions. When project leaders offered to write a final summary, they were emphatically told, "No more reports! We want to make sense of it ourselves." The planning committee articulated a clear and compelling meeting purpose: to discuss the findings in reference to the project goals and objectives and to determine areas of agreement. This became the foundation for an aggressive agenda that would allow the roundtable to exchange perspectives and strive for agreement.

At the second planning committee meeting, the facilitators tested the design, simulating aspects of the actual synthesis session. After this rehearsal, everyone was more confident that the synthesis workshops had a good chance of success. The run-through especially buoyed the confidence of the DOT staffer on the committee. Understandably, he worried whether the roundtable could ever reach agreement. Accustomed to playing an expert role and choosing the best option as part of a technical team, he doubted the value of the synthesis meetings. The practice run helped him see the possibility of meaningful discussion and of reaching real agreement.

The Synthesis Workshops

The synthesis workshops used small groups for most of the discussions. Partners were intentionally placed in groups with very diverse opinions. People participated actively. One roundtable member said, "Sitting in the small groups, we were forced to work things out with people we would not necessarily talk to otherwise. I quickly realized we had a lot in common." Prejudices and stereotypes began to dissolve.

The workshops were tightly choreographed so small groups focused on one clear, meaningful task at a time. Small groups moved to different tasks and gave input on all matters. Beginning with the roundtable's original goals and objectives, first they spoke about the goals they each cared about most. Later, they used all the goals as criteria to evaluate the various road options. During these discussions, they identified areas of possible agreement.

The workshops built shared understanding before trying to make any decisions. People realized they all cared about their neighborhoods, the traffic, and the environment. As the workshop progressed, trust grew. Small groups identified points of possible agreement and posted them as they emerged.

Eventually it was time to see which points could become full group agreements. The facilitators conducted this as a full group session focusing on areas of easy agreement first. When an idea drew a lot of controversy, it was put aside. By focusing where there was agreement, a lot was accomplished, and hopefulness predominated.

In the end, there was strong agreement on most aspects of a solution. Support grew for an innovative option that put Route 1 in a "cut" below street level. This would allow the three notorious traffic lights to be removed and speed travel along the main road. The three local cross streets would remain at normal street level, passing above Route 1, their cultural and environmental resources intact. Other small connector roads were planned, although the bypass near the river remained controversial and did not become part of the agreement.

At last, a workable compromise had been found. While the Route-1-in-a-cut solution may not have provided the most optimal relief from traffic congestion, it provided adequate relief. It accomplished this while accommodating the other myriad goals. Many participants reported that these intense working synthesis sessions were among the most satisfying moments of the entire roundtable process.

Results

The solution preferred by the Partners' Roundtable has become the officially sanctioned solution. That decision was made by DOT in consultation with the project team after the synthesis workshops. NJDOT submitted the EIS, and the Federal Highway Administration adopted it in a formal record of decision. It has progressed to the design stage at NJDOT. To date, no challenges have been filed against the proposal. This alone represents a very significant measure of success.

Lessons Learned

Change the Structure, Change the Outcome

Shifting the structure of public participation enabled the roundtable members to move from advocacy to collaboration. The DOT was no longer the hub of the communication wheel, stuck trying to reconcile competing interests. Instead, the agency became part of the circle of collaborators. The citizen and institutional stakeholders were no longer on the outside lobbing their concerns in; they were part of the circle seeking a solution.

The Power of Small Groups

The roundtable made the most progress in building trust and agreement when participants interacted in small groups on specific tasks. The membership committee, the goals and objectives committee, and the planning committee for the synthesis workshops were small, task-focused groups that produced results and functioned very well. The synthesis workshops themselves were mostly a series of small group meetings on specific tasks. The small group structure allowed people to get beyond stereotypes, have meaningful conversations, and find common ground.

Long-Term Community Building

Even in this extremely polarized group, the methods in this project allowed people to find common ground and, in some cases, became ongoing collaborators. One member recalled how she and another woman had "dagger eyes for each other" until they worked together in a small group at the synthesis workshops. They had been trapped in stereotypes but quickly found common ground. "I realized she cared about her neighborhood just as I did," she said. Since then, they have cooperated to change a dangerous section of road where fatal accidents had occurred. As a result of this unprecedented engagement experience, this community has increased its capacity for future collaboration.

Adopt a Facilitative Leadership Stance

Facilitation was a high priority for the project team. Martin and Jon consciously facilitated a learning process, both within the roundtable and within the project team. Facilitation ensured that information and opinions were shared openly, that meetings were focused, and that understanding and agreements were reached. Jon Carnegie noted that at first it was tough to step aside from his professional judgment on solutions or approaches. But as he said, "My job was not to express my opinion as a transportation planner but to facilitate the delivery of that information and facilitate the deliberations."

Stay Grounded in Goals

Discussing and agreeing on goals built understanding of the situation and of the project's aims. It allowed real collaboration as people listened to each other, produced something of value, and built true commitment to the goals. In this case, the goals and objectives became critical in evaluating and selecting a solution.

Build Agreement Step by Step

One DOT manager reported that from this experience he has learned to break projects into pieces and build agreement step by step. He now applies this principle to all his projects, first reaching agreement on purpose and scope before delving into the details of goals. Groups work more effectively when they build understanding of a situation before attempting to make decisions.

Transparency Levels the Playing Field

A completely transparent process can shift the established balance of power. For instance, elected officials and state agencies are usually granted formal authority while environmental and neighborhood groups too often have less formal influence or are limited to protesting after the fact. But power at the roundtable was given to those who showed up and participated, not just to those in positions of power. Transparency of data and process meant all agreements were made with all the stakeholder groups in the room.

Conclusion

Engaging the full range of stakeholders in a complex decision-making process may seem cumbersome and overly time-consuming. Nevertheless, when there is a great deal of controversy and a need for stakeholder support, a robust engagement process is a more efficient way to get real results. Protest and lack of agreement had stalled progress on a Route 1 fix for years. As a result of the Partners' Roundtable, there is now a clear mandate on a path forward.

Amy Steffen is an organizational development consultant. (*amysteffen@ verizon.net*)Lonnie Weiss, president of Weiss Consulting, LLC, is a certified professional facilitator. (*lonnie@weissconsults.com*)

VI. THE SCOOP INITIATIVE

Patrick Sanaghan, Francis E. Blanco, and Samuel Frisby

Challenge: Creating a cross-boundary youth services program including city agencies and diverse community providers

Introduction

TRENTON, NEW JERSEY, is a small northeastern city with a population of roughly eighty-five thousand people, eighteen thousand of whom are school-aged youth (grades K-12). It is a city with a strong sense of territoriality that is both historic and deep. In the past, this mind-set has prevented collaboration and cooperation across neighborhoods and among service providers.

Trenton has four political wards (i.e., north, south, east, and west) that may seem to an outsider like four smaller cities, each with its own unique culture, demographics, opportunities, and history. People often are more proud of their ward than they are of the city as a whole.

Trenton residents tend to be protective of resources, are suspicious of outsiders, and take care of their own. Cooperation, when it happens, is opportunistic rather than long-term. In many ways, this sense of territoriality has not served Trenton's citizens well.

This case study is about how an integrated, collaborative service program for youth called Social Celebrations, Organizations, Opportunities, and People (SCOOP) was created and implemented throughout the city.

As a result of this collaborative initiative, the Mayor's Youth Advocacy Cabinet of Trenton received the national City Livability Award in 2005 from the U.S. Conference of Mayors.

The Youth Summit

In 2001, Trenton Mayor Douglas Palmer convened the first citywide youth summit for all the youth service providers in the city. He asked the school superintendent and the City of Trenton Department of Recreation, Natural Resources, and Culture (DRNR&C) to co-sponsor this historic event. The primary purpose of this summit was to create a more integrated and coherent network for youth services throughout the city.

Several factors called for this kind of summit. First, money from the federal government was dwindling, forcing service providers to compete with each other for limited slices of the pie. Many service providers were offering redundant programs for youth (e.g., there were lots of basketball programs). The youth were further underserved by the limited number of available programs, and programs did not reflect their interests or needs. Finally, many young people could not participate in quality programs due to transportation, communication, and security issues.

The superintendent asked a trusted consultant with experience in collaborative practices and strategic planning to help plan and facilitate the daylong event. The consultant met several times with representatives from the school district and DRNR&C to plan and design the summit.

The initial youth summit was designed to be highly interactive and participative and involved over one hundred service providers as well as ten youth representatives. During the day, three major themes were explored:

- *Past.* Summit participants looked at *past* efforts to provide meaningful programs for youth and distilled some lessons learned.
- *Present.* They did a strengths, weaknesses, opportunities, threats (SWOT) analysis of current programs for youth.
- *Future.* They created a future picture or preferred future of what an integrated network for youth services might look like for the city.

The day was designed to involve everyone and hear all the voices and perspectives, *especially* the students. It became apparent to participants that they had to collaborate with each other if they were to reach their shared aspirations. They committed themselves to creating a planning process over the next year that would move them toward more integration and coherence.

Surveys

As planning for the initial youth summit was taking place, there were also two surveys being conducted, one by the DRNR&C and another by the College of New Jersey, a local university in Trenton. The goal was to create a comprehensive assessment of all programs available to youth throughout the city. This was done by individual surveys, focus groups, visiting programs, talking with youth, and knocking on a lot of doors.

After nearly a year, both surveys were completed, offering a detailed snapshot of all available programs. This was the first time the city had such an accurate and comprehensive picture of youth services in Trenton.

Among many important findings, three factors stood out:

- At the time of the surveys, *females* represented only 10 percent of participants in youth programs throughout the city.
- One ward had most of the programs. Not surprisingly, *the most affluent ward* was well served while the less affluent wards were vastly underserved.
- The *types of programs* available did not meet the diverse needs and interests of the youth, so participation was low throughout the city.

Mini-summits

After the initial youth summit, the DRNR&C director conducted a series of mini-summits in the city's four wards to solicit feedback on the summit findings and seek advice about what kind of programs parents and youth wanted in their neighborhoods. Hundreds of citizens participated in these mini-summits.

After the summit was over, the surveys completed, and the feedback rounds conducted, the planning consultant was charged with creating a report that would identify explicit next steps toward creating "an integrated network for youth services" throughout the city. In a collaborative dialogue with the school superintendent and the DRNR&C director, the consultant wrote a white paper that made several strong recommendations. These recommendations detailed the collaborative *mechanisms* needed to create a citywide integrated network for youth services.

The superintendent, DRNR&C director, and consultant then met with the mayor to discuss the proposed plan and gain his approval; at the end of the meeting, the mayor told the group, *"You need to make this happen as soon as possible."*

SCOOP is Born

The mayor agreed to create and co-chair a youth task group. This high-level group meets *quarterly* to discuss strategy, set policy, and make any difficult decisions affecting the city's young people (e.g., resource allocation). The group's primary responsibility is to look across the city to ensure access, equity, and availability of quality programs for all youth, and its meetings are facilitated by the outside planning consultant.

In addition to the mayor, the group includes the police chief, president of the Trenton Board of Education and superintendent, the director of the Housing Authority, the president of City Council, the director of Health and Human Services, the provost of a local college, the president of the county United Way, the DRNR&C director, and a highly respected member of the clergy.

The mayor also created an operations council consisting of staff who report directly to members of the youth task group. This council takes the recommendations from the higher-level group and *implements* them. This group is co-chaired by an assistant superintendent of schools and the DRNR&C director and meets *monthly* at the school district's administrative office.

The first important responsibility of the youth task group was to identify their key representative to the operations council. The planning consultant communicated to the mayor that this would be the most important decision to be made. The right people *had* to be assigned to operations, or the initiative would fail. They could not settle for the "usual suspects" or people with some time on their hands. This had to be seen as a primary responsibility for highly qualified and motivated individuals.

Editors Note: *One of the challenges of collaborative and cross-boundary work is selecting the right people for the right task. Too often, volunteers or well-intentioned people who want to help just aren't the right people for the job at hand. It takes discipline to choose the appropriate individuals and not get swept up with enthusiasm and pick people who are merely interested in helping.*

Several important criteria for members of the operations council were negotiated and agreed upon by members of the youth task group. Then each member nominated a staff person for the operations council who they could hold accountable and who met the established criteria:

- *They had to be decision makers.* The operations members have the power to make decisions with direct implications for their own organizations. We wanted to avoid the "I have to check with my boss before I can commit" syndrome.
- *They had to be "players."* These members had to have both the skills and reputation for getting things done. This was not a think tank or group of theorists.

- *They had to be savvy.* These members had to understand how to deal with the behind-the-scenes stuff that regulates most complex organizations. In any city, there are complexities around turf issues, departmental cultures, politics, power, history, etc.
- *They had to be collaborative.* They had to be able to work with others in a team approach. They were given little glory but a lot of work to do. These members could not be cowboys or lone wolves.

The mayor charged the DRNR&C director to be the "owner" of this collaborative, citywide effort and identified her department as the lead agency that would facilitate implementation of the SCOOP initiative. He promised to provide the necessary resources and support to help make SCOOP successful and clearly communicated that he would hold the director accountable for the results. SCOOP was on its way!

Putting the Operational Structures in Place

In the first year of the SCOOP initiative, the operations council created three key operating mechanisms that helped support the integrated network and sustain the collaborative efforts of service providers throughout the city.

The SCOOP Web Page

Historically, the city government published a booklet every few years that identified available programs for youth. It was often incomplete and obsolete before it was printed and distributed. This had to change.

To improve matters, the DRNR&C and the school district worked together to produce a user-friendly, informative Web page that fully describes all the programs and services available for youth throughout the city. The SCOOP Web site is linked to both the school district's Web page as well as the city's.

The Web page was designed by students (elementary, middle, and high school) and allows any student, parent, or guardian to look up programs and choose their educational and recreational experiences. The selections are categorized by neighborhood, date, location, or program. Student focus groups provide ongoing feedback about the Web page content, usability, and relevance. It is continually updated by service providers, and they have put safeguards and protocols in place to ensure timely and accurate information.

Transportation System

At the initial summit, it was discovered that even if Trenton had great programs for youth, many could not get to them. There is a very limited public transportation system in Trenton, and many families do not own cars.

The youth task group charged the operations team with creating a safe, reliable, and free transportation system allowing access to any program site. It took about a year to research and organize all the issues involved in the creation of a transportation service, including communication, insurance, scheduling, union rules, and safety.

The operations team worked closely with the school district (which had buses) to deal effectively with each issue. It also leased some buses from local churches.

The team created a shuttle service to all program sites. Each bus has a certified driver and bus aide. They use a walkie-talkie system to communicate between buses. A centralized radio system links all buses with a central office and SCOOP sites. Police monitor communication, conduct daily site inspections, and follow the buses to ensure safety and communicate to the community their strong support of the programs.

The Student Identification System

When the parents were asked about their greatest concerns regarding SCOOP, the safety of their children was at the very top of their list. If they were going to entrust their children to the program, they had to make sure they would be safe within each program site and *especially* while being transported to and from the programs.

The SCOOP team was charged with creating and implementing a student tracking system. The operations council invested in a technology-based program that would be able to monitor students throughout the program network. It was the biggest up-front investment of the entire SCOOP initiative, but the team strongly believed that if they were to establish a long-term, integrated network, it was essential to make the investment in technology.

A registration process was instituted that obtained parental/guardian permission to participate in SCOOP programs. Each registered youth received a laminated photo ID with technology chips embedded in them. These ID cards have the student's name, address, and school.

Each student who comes to a SCOOP site has their ID scanned into a database before they are allowed to participate in any programs. This allows tracking of the student at all times. It can be determined where a student is within three minutes even if they are on a bus halfway across the city.

If parents/guardians don't want their child participating at a specific program site, this is encoded into their ID card, and they will not be allowed to disembark at that site.

A Current Snapshot, 2006-2007

1. There are thirteen SCOOP sites with over five thousand students registered and participating in over one hundred programs throughout the city. (This is triple the number of students before the SCOOP initiative was launched.) The services are from 3:30 p.m. until 9:00 p.m., five days a week and include Saturdays from 9:00 a.m. until 2:00 p.m.
2. Youth summits are conducted yearly to bring together all the service providers in the city. The purpose of these all-day meetings is to share progress toward stated goals, identify problems and challenges, share information across different systems, and create new programs and initiatives. These are designed to be highly participative and engaging. The mayor attends these summits.
3. Youth forums for teens are conducted every year and involve seventy-five to one hundred youth throughout the city of Trenton. They are careful not to just invite the "choir" to this important meeting and work hard to ensure that a broad diversity of students participates. These forums are professionally facilitated by members of the operations council and a professor from the College of New Jersey. These forums create real-time data to key questions affecting youth. Each student receives a summary of their day's work *before* they leave the meeting.

   The primary purpose of these forums is to listen to the concerns of the youth. The information generated informs the yearly youth summits. Teen representatives from the forum make formal presentations and recommendations at the youth summits. These recommendations have resulted in meaningful changes in program design, quality, and access.
   To build in accountability, the director of DRNR&C attends the youth forums and reports back to them what has been done to address their previous year's concerns and aspirations.

It is very important that, as leaders, we listen to our youth and create programs that meet their interests and needs. The information that is created in the yearly youth forums not only helps inform our thinking but holds us accountable for responding to their issues and concerns.

—Mayor Douglas Palmer, 2006

4. In the initial stages of SCOOP, recreation sites and schools were utilized as primary program sites. There are many organizations in Trenton that provide quality programs for youth (e.g., CYO, YMCA, Boys and Girls Club, the 4H Club, Girl Scouts, etc.), and many have their own buildings to conduct their programs. The director of DRNR&C and the members of SCOOP have reached out to interested parties and expanded the SCOOP network to include nine new partners and nine new sites. This is the next phase of the integrated network. These external partners meet monthly with the head of the Division of Recreation (who reports to the director of DRNR&C) to share information, solve problems, build relationships, and connect with each other.

Each "partner" must agree to several nonnegotiable criteria before participating in the SCOOP initiative. For example, (1) the organization must be willing to provide programming for any of the youth participating in SCOOP, (2) it must have adequate security and safety measures in place including background checks of all personnel, (3) it must utilize the SCOOP photo ID system, and (4) it must provide some free programming to SCOOP participants (some of these organizations charge for programs), etc.

Lessons on Collaboration from SCOOP

Creating a shared picture of the future is essential.

Instead of the city administration *telling* youth service providers to collaborate or *selling* their own vision and goals, they created the opportunity for stakeholders to articulate their own shared vision and aspirations. The initial summit in 2001 was highly inclusive and allowed everyone's ideas to be voiced *and* heard. No individual or small group was allowed to dominate the discussions no matter how powerful they were.

With over one hundred participants, the team focused on common-ground ideas yet acknowledged meaningful differences. Discovering the common ground was very powerful because stakeholders began to see the natural connections to their work and their shared aspirations for youth. Common ground creates the foundation for action and allows different views to be considered, discussed, and resolved *over time*. A shared picture creates its own motivation and momentum and builds both responsibility and ownership for its realization.

You have to keep your word.

After the initial summit, the team made several promises to the youth providers throughout the city and the school district. They have upheld their commitments, creating a sense of trust throughout the city. The SCOOP "brand" is highly trusted.

The team promised that it would share all the information created at both the youth summits and the youth forum with all the service providers. Complete transparency is the goal. It also committed to holding yearly youth summits and youth forums. This has happened for the last five years. Finally, it promised to create a transparent communication vehicle for all the SCOOP programs. Every service provider can share information about its programs and services to everyone in the city through the SCOOP Web site.

Relationships matter.

This may well be the most powerful lesson of all. In cross-boundary, collaborative work, problems and challenges are unavoidable. It is essential to build meaningful relationships with everyone throughout the initiative. When a problem does arise, you can then bring the right people together to help solve the problem and *not* blame each other. When there is mutual respect in the professional relationships, people will stretch a little to answer that e-mail or phone call quickly and lend a hand or a resource because they know you as a person, and most importantly, they trust you.

Relationship building takes time, patience, and authenticity, but the payoff is worth the investment. Most plans look great on paper, but it is people who implement them. Pay attention to relationships.

You have to stay at the table.

When you are trying to organize something as complicated as SCOOP, there are hundreds of details and plenty of hurdles along the way; after the big ideas are created, someone has to do the difficult work. Much of this is detailed, even tedious, but someone has to do it.

If things get difficult, people have to be willing to stay and resolve the differences. This takes patience, tenacity, and the willingness to listen. When you are working with bureaucratic systems with their unique structures, cultures, histories, and ways of doing things, you have to understand their complexities. This takes time, persistence, and care.

Leadership has to pay attention to the process.

In a multiyear effort, it is easy to lose focus and create the next bigger and better initiative. The three key leaders (the mayor, the school superintendent, and the DRNR&C director) all paid attention to this complex initiative. The mayor attends all youth task group meetings. The superintendent is always available for support, important meetings, strategizing, and problem solving. He talks about SCOOP in faculty meetings, with the community, and at board meetings. The director has communicated to internal and external stakeholders that this is a top priority for her department. All three model the way as the participants continue building this initiative.

Symbolism is important.

When the mayor convened the first youth summit, he insisted that the school superintendent and the DRNR&C director cosponsor the meeting. He wanted them to model collaboration and partnership from the very beginning. The youth task force is cochaired by the mayor *and* the director, demonstrating to the top leaders that this is an important initiative.

The client has to be in the room.

In collaborative work, you don't plan *for* someone, you plan *with* someone. With SCOOP, the youth were our clients. To create the best programs for Trenton youth, we *asked* them for program ideas. We *involved* them in the youth summits along with adults. Their ideas, suggestions, and recommendations *influenced* decision making and policy, and they are consistently surveyed about program quality and design. They believe they have a say in the matter.

It helps to have power.

The fact that the mayor was personally involved and championed this effort throughout its creation and implementation was critical to the success of SCOOP.

The mayor signaled by word and deed that this initiative was important to him. This enabled the city departments to coordinate and cooperate across their "silos" and political boundaries. There was little bickering or posturing because it was clear what the mayor wanted.

The mayor had the power to call all the relevant parties to the table when needed. He chaired and led the quarterly meetings and convened special meetings when necessary. Not surprisingly, attendance at these meetings was *very* high.

At the top-level meetings, all the top administrators are at the table; no seconds are allowed. When they leave the quarterly meetings, they are very clear on what needs to be done. They communicate this to their staff, and collaborative *implementation* occurs.

A "no blame" stance enables learning when things go wrong.

In the initial dry run of the shuttle bus system, we asked task group and operations team members to ride with us, along with some older students. The goal was to work out the kinks . . . . , and there were plenty to work out. There were glitches with communication, schedules, even finding the right recreation sites. You name it, we experienced it.

We had planned for a debriefing session to identify problems and solve them. We only had two hours to do a full debrief, and we weren't looking forward to it because we believed that people would be critical of one another. In light of this, we articulated a "no blame" stance. We emphasized that the purpose of the meeting was to solve problems, not criticize each other.

There were thirty participants in the meeting, and the facilitator put people into several mixed groups and had them identify several problems. Each group reported out what they believed was a problem to be solved, and a master list was created in front of the whole group.

Participants were then given the opportunity to choose the problems they wanted to work on and come up with solutions. No one blamed anyone else for a problem. People focused on solving the problem and moving things forward. It was amazing to see people working together, proactively and positively, to create real solutions. A moral victory had been achieved. That meeting set a tone for the future and communicated to everyone that the purpose was to solve problems together, not point fingers. That tone permeates SCOOP meetings even today. The next week, hundreds of students were safely transported.

Patrick Sanaghan is president of the Sanaghan group (*sanaghan@aol.com*). Francis E. Blanco is former director of the City of Trenton Department of Recreation, Natural Resources and Culture (DRNR&C) and is currently director of the New Jersey Department of the Treasury, Division of Minority and Women Business Development (*Francis.Blanco@treas.state.nj.us*). Samuel Frisby is Trenton's current director of DRNR&C (*sfrisby@trentonnj.org*).

VII. NATURE UNDER PRESSURE

Jeff Marshall and Sharon Young

Challenge: Helping property owners and municipalities preserve threatened open spaces through collaboration

Introduction

S INCE 1958 THE Heritage Conservancy has preserved thousands of acres of land and dozens of historic sites and has completed many watershed plans, river and open-space plans, and feasibility studies. The Heritage Conservancy is an acknowledged leader in land and historic preservation throughout eastern Pennsylvania and central-west New Jersey.

What is a Lasting Landscape?

Every day our beautiful natural areas; vast open spaces; and rich, historic heritage enhance our living environment and help create a "sense of place." They provide an intrinsic feeling of belonging and permanence. In recognition of and respect for our natural and historic resources and to ensure that these places are preserved for future generations, the Heritage Conservancy created the Lasting Landscapes initiative in 1999.

The initiative is designed as a comprehensive and collaborative approach to conserving landscapes that are both scientifically and historically significant and treasured by their local communities.

A Lasting Landscape may be a relatively small area of concentrated natural, cultural, or historical resources or a large area within a regional context, such as a watershed. These special places allow people to interact with the natural environment and contribute to our physical and emotional health; historic sites preserve our culture and heritage as well as add charm and character to our surroundings. The loss of these properties would irrevocably damage the character of communities.

The Heritage Conservancy has established seven Lasting Landscapes since 1999, and this case study will describe in detail the collaborative approach of this initiative as well as highlight several projects of particular interest and importance.

Building a Coalition

It is important to mention at the outset that implementation of the Lasting Landscapes approach requires local organizational commitment on the part of any community group, nonprofit organization, governmental body, or consortium of such groups. This is a comprehensive approach to natural and historic resource protection that requires the collaborative support and expertise of resource protection specialists, community planners, and stewardship professionals representing all of these disciplines. Therefore, the Heritage Conservancy established a staff team for each lasting landscape, along with a staff leader who is responsible for shepherding the project through each step and ensuring its success.

In addition to a staff team, there must be strong community representation and involvement in forming a local leadership team. Without an effective leadership team, the Lasting Landscapes approach will fail. These dedicated volunteers help with many of the practical, mission-critical jobs associated with a Lasting Landscape, from securing funds to getting local media coverage. The leadership team also provides continuing knowledge about the community's priorities and needs.

The leadership team should represent the major constituencies in a Lasting Landscape area, which usually includes the business community, grassroots conservation and community service groups, local governmental bodies, and individual community leaders. The ideal size of a leadership team is between twelve and fifteen individuals, with one person serving as chairperson.

Members of the leadership team and the team chairperson must be chosen carefully. Ideally, they will serve as true partners to the staff team and play a major part in securing vital funding for projects. These individuals need to both understand and be committed to the Lasting Landscape's goals, and they must be able to represent and serve as ambassadors to the community.

A Four-Step Process

Creating a Lasting Landscape involves a comprehensive four-step process that identifies a landscape for preservation and establishes the infrastructure to work effectively with local communities. The goal is to work in partnership with communities to protect, preserve, and care for the important and valuable resources of that area in perpetuity.

The four steps are the following:

1. *Research*
2. *Planning*
3. *Implementation*
4. *Stewardship*

These steps comprise a thoughtful and disciplined approach to complex, cross-boundary work with communities. *How they are implemented* makes all the difference in the world. The common thread running through the entire process is the collaborative community effort that keeps preservation efforts and projects moving, from the initial identification of key resources to the preservation and stewardship of the resources.

This collaborative, community-based approach has worked in several very different environments. In the next sections, you will read brief descriptions of several Lasting Landscapes that the Heritage Conservancy staff and leadership have been involved in over the last several years.

The Forks of the Neshaminy

It all started in the lovely Rushland area of Bucks County. Also known as the Forks of the Neshaminy because its lush stream valleys are formed by the juncture of the Neshaminy and Little Neshaminy Creeks, this area is dotted with historic sites among rolling agricultural fields.

In the 1980s and '90s, Heritage Conservancy developed a strong presence in the Forks of the Neshaminy. These included surveying and documenting the area's historical features and recommending it as a rural historic district. The Heritage Conservancy also worked with a group of neighboring Warwick Township landowners to preserve open space and agricultural land. It also acquired the beautiful, 200-acre Lindsay Farm and began planning restoration and adaptive reuse projects there. There was simultaneously a growing awareness of preservation in the area as evidenced by Warwick Township's 1999 Open Space Plan, which identified the protection of natural resources and the preservation of agricultural soils as the township's first and second priorities, respectively.

Two events transformed these individual efforts into a larger project that would become the first Lasting Landscape. First, the area was recognized in the 1998 Natural Areas Inventory of Bucks County as containing significant natural features that should receive priority for protection.

Second, the Gemmill family asked Heritage Conservancy to create a conservation plan for their nearly four hundred acres of property in Warwick Township, which includes Five Spruce Farm. This is one of the largest privately held, undeveloped parcels in Bucks County and includes woodlands, working farm fields, and historic farmsteads. The conservancy's research indicated that the long-term sustainability of this farm and the ability to preserve it depended on surrounding properties remaining in agricultural use as well. The Heritage Conservancy had to face the fact that preserving even this large, enormously valuable property would not in itself be a long-term conservation victory. It would need to think bigger.

The conservancy began hosting meetings on conservation of historic and natural resources for neighbors and township and county officials. To help spread the word, it also prepared a document titled "Lasting Landscapes—a Concept for the Preservation of the Natural and Historic Features of the Forks of the Neshaminy." The idea caught on that a window of opportunity still existed to effectively preserve the remaining significant natural and man-made features across this landscape.

The conservancy set about documenting and mapping the area's natural and historic features, agricultural soils, and scenic vistas. The Forks of the Neshaminy watershed, while primarily located in Warwick Township, spans 5,600 acres in four townships, so officials from the different municipalities were brought together to begin thinking about and planning conservation. With input from officials and community members, specific conservation goals and strategies were identified.

"If we don't protect it now, we will lose it forever," stated Bill Brasko, a Warwick Township resident and conservationist.

The conservancy then began implementing the conservation plan, with a schedule, task assignments, and fund-raising goals for resource protection projects. In partnership with municipal open space or environmental advisory committees, it coordinated many meetings with individual property owners to educate them on land-use options and the various land and historic preservation tools and techniques available to them. The conservancy also sought and provided matching funds for county and state acquisition of properties and easements.

The landscape-level approach to conservation in the Forks of the Neshaminy has been enormously successful. The conservancy owns or has otherwise preserved nearly six hundred acres in the Lasting Landscape and has made deep connections to the community that will be valuable as it continues to preserve land and influence both conservation policy and private practice.

The Quakertown Swamp Trail: Planning for Conservation and Community

The 518-acre Quakertown Swamp is a natural treasure for Bucks County, Pennsylvania, and the entire Delaware Valley region. It is one of the largest freshwater inland wetlands in southeastern Pennsylvania. In addition to being the home of the largest great blue heron rookery in eastern Pennsylvania, the swamp supports seventy-three other bird species, including several rare breeders, and has been designated by the National Audubon Society as one of seventy important bird areas in the state.

Like all wetlands, the swamp provides many important practical benefits to the human community. Its dense plant growth absorbs pollutants from water, thus protecting water quality for a large portion of Bucks County, and it helps prevent flooding by serving as a natural rainwater storage basin. Continued development in and around the swamp could affect water levels, flooding, and habitat in this valuable natural area.

In 2000 the Quakertown Swamp was designated as a Lasting Landscape. During the research phase, the conservancy identified the most important individual resources that needed protection. In the planning phase, it devised protection strategies including purchasing or placing conservation easements on key properties and identifying ways to engage the public with the swamp, thereby building support for the implementation and stewardship that would follow.

From the start, it was evident that, in addition to and because of its innate and unique natural value, the swamp offered enormous potential for public education and participation. However, the largest portion of the land that comprises Quakertown Swamp is private property, a fact that made both educational and overall conservation efforts much more complicated. It was clear to all involved that more public accessibility would mean more public engagement. And so the idea of a Quakertown Swamp Trail was born. Shortly thereafter, the conservancy began developing plans for a trail network in consultation with others. These plans culminated in a collaborative agreement between the conservancy and the township to construct a trail network that would begin on township property and extend into and through Conservancy-owned lands with the potential for expansion in the future.

By 2002 the Heritage Conservancy had acquired two important properties in the swamp, totaling about seventy acres. Richland Township, a local government, had purchased an adjacent eleven-acre parcel. Working closely with federal, state, county, and local agencies, as well as the leadership team and the trails committee, the conservancy helped craft a trail plan that provides public access to and showcases the swamp's many important attributes without having an adverse impact on them. Importantly, the plan allows for phased implementation as funding becomes available.

The Bats of Durham

Historically, the Durham Bat Mine was once the home of the Durham Furnace and Iron Works, established in 1727, which produced shot and shells for Washington's revolutionary army and operated into the late 1800s. The five mines that once produced much of the iron and limestone for the Durham Iron Works were largely forgotten for decades.

By the 1930s, people began to realize that one of the abandoned mines, which has since become known as the Durham Bat Mine, had become an important bat hibernaculum (a place where bats hibernate over the winter). Nevertheless, the mine was generally considered a nuisance and a public health hazard. After several major and well-publicized rescues of would-be adventurers, there was an understandable public outcry to bulldoze the mine entrance.

In 1994 Heritage Conservancy spearheaded an effort to simultaneously prevent the destruction of the bat habitat and tackle the very real human safety issue by installing "bat-friendly" gates that would prevent people, but not bats, from getting in and out of the mine.

From that time on, Heritage paid close attention to the 150-acre critical habitat area surrounding the Durham Bat Mine, which is located in the Cooks Creek Watershed. Studies in the 1990s indicated just how significant a natural resource the mine is: it is the second largest bat hibernaculum in Pennsylvania and is home to as many as ten thousand bats each winter. Bats play an important role in the ecosystem by, among other things, controlling insect populations that would otherwise plague farmers, foresters, and the general public.

In 2000 the conservancy designated the Cooks Creek Watershed—a first priority site in the Bucks County Natural Areas Inventory and home to many important natural and historic resources—as a Lasting Landscape. The conservancy knew that the fascinating story and natural value of the watershed's signature property, the Durham Bat Mine, would be a huge boon to overall conservation efforts in the area and that the comprehensive strategies applied to the new Lasting Landscape would benefit the mine as well.

How does this mutual benefit work? On one hand, no natural resource exists in a vacuum. The best preserved and most ideal hibernaculum in the world can't protect a bat population that lacks a safe, clean environment in which to eat, mate, and raise young in spring and summer. The conservancy's work in the Cooks Creek Watershed—identifying important natural resources, acquiring them or placing easements on them, and helping municipalities and nonprofit organizations create eco-friendly plans—added layers of protection to the bat habitat. For example, the Watershed Association has participated in such bat-related projects as the 2004 telemetry project, in which bats leaving the hibernaculum were banded and tracked to determine their summer flight, roosting, and foraging patterns.

On the other hand, the bat mine has often been a key selling point for the entire Lasting Landscape, which has helped secure public, private, and government support and funding to protect other important sites in the Cooks Creek Watershed. The fact that these sites are part of the Durham bat's critical habitat or that they support the habitat enormously strengthens the conservancy's efforts—and its grant applications.

The Durham bats and their famous adopted home have captured the public imagination like few other natural resources in the Cooks Creek Watershed or the entire region have. Outreach activities like the Creatures of the Night and Flight and Fantasy in the Night programs have attracted many families who might not normally attend conservation-related events. The conservancy has used these occasions, along with public bat-box-building events, to teach not only about bats and the great services they provide but also about the terrible effects of disappearing wildlife habitat, the larger Cooks Creek Watershed, and the effort to preserve its natural and historic resources.

Land trusts never work alone. Their success relies heavily on the involvement, participation, and support of many local groups, government agencies, and concerned citizens who have chosen to make conservation the highest priority.

Other Lasting Landscapes

The following are brief snapshots of other Lasting Landscapes that show the diverse range of initiatives this approach can support.

Musconetcong River Valley Lasting Landscapes Watershed

The forty-two-mile-long Musconetcong River is the largest nontidal tributary to the Delaware River in New Jersey. It was designated as a Wild and Scenic River in 2006. Wild and Scenic River designation places a layer of protection on a river as a valued natural resource; it also makes federal funds for resource conservation projects, such as bank stabilization, more easily available.

Heritage Conservancy played an important role in achieving this milestone. In June 2004, the conservancy completed the Musconetcong River National Wild and Scenic Rivers Study on behalf of the Musconetcong Watershed Association. This study, which was funded by the National Parks Service, determined which river segments were eligible for inclusion in the national system and identified appropriate classifications for the segments so designated. In addition, Heritage Conservancy staff participated in advisory committee meetings and facilitated public meetings associated with this project.

Route 113 Heritage Corridor Lasting Landscapes

Route 113 began as a transportation and cultural link to the Germanic farming communities surrounding Philadelphia from the Delaware River to the Schuylkill River. Spanning more than thirty miles and traversing the counties of Bucks and Montgomery in Pennsylvania, the Route 113 Heritage Corridor includes historic towns, rolling hills, and green lands. Today, this important roadway is under significant pressure from advancing suburbanization.

Heritage Conservancy is working with municipalities and local leadership to develop a sustainability plan that will serve as a roadmap for long-term stewardship of natural and heritage resources in the Route 113 corridor. Building on existing documents, the project will create a baseline understanding of corridorwide conservation needs, prioritize natural and historic resource conservation needs along the corridor, develop an integrated corridorwide strategic direction for conservation activities, and engage the community in understanding and addressing long-term sustainability needs within the corridor. The project will provide an integrated planning document for local municipalities and conservation organizations as well as a comprehensive guide for regional and state greenway and heritage park planners.

Pidcock Creek

Pidcock Creek is a small tributary of the Delaware River, which serves as an important drinking water source for both Camden and Philadelphia. The creek is over 6.5 miles long and drains an area of approximately 12.7 square miles in the Bucks County townships of Buckingham, Upper Makefield, Solebury, and Wrightstown.

Although it was not officially designated a Lasting Landscape until 2006, Heritage Conservancy has been working to preserve land in the Pidcock Creek watershed for the past twenty years. Through collaborative associations with municipalities and landowners in the region, the conservancy has assisted in the preservation of a critical mass of land in this significant region.

Bushkill Creek Watershed Lasting Landscape

The Bushkill Creek Watershed encompasses eighty square miles of Northampton County, Pennsylvania, stretching from Blue Mountain to the Delaware River in Easton. Groundwater recharge along the wooded slopes of Blue Mountain provides high-quality water for the headwaters of Bushkill Creek. Wetlands along the foot of the mountain also help to buffer the streams from surface runoff while providing important wildlife habitat.

The Bushkill Stream Conservancy played a key role in the development of the Two Rivers Area Greenway Plan, commissioned by the Two Rivers Council of Governments, which served as a blueprint for conservation and recreation projects in the watershed. In 2004 the Bushkill Stream Conservancy asked Heritage Conservancy to join a greenway partnership. A partnership made up of the Bushkill Stream Conservancy, Heritage Conservancy, and Wildlands Conservancy joined with county and municipal officials, two bureaus of the Pennyslvania Department of Conservation and Natural Resources (DCNR), and the Delaware and Lehigh Heritage Corridor to advance common conservation projects. This group meets regularly and serves as a "local leadership team."

Lessons Learned

An outside organization cannot effect change within a community.

To be successful, Heritage Conservancy had to develop long-term relationships with key stakeholders. Just as importantly, they had to listen to input from the community. The conservancy developed a philosophy of going in with good science and then listening carefully to good people in order to develop mutual trust with community leaders and property owners.

A highly competent community-based leadership team is essential to the success of Lasting Landscape. In the end, the community has to own both the process and the outcomes. Outsiders cannot create a Lasting Landscape; only the community can do this. Organizations like the Heritage Conservancy can help facilitate the process, provide technical expertise, and lend their experience. But in the end, the community's ownership is key, and the leadership team helps build that sense of ownership.

Authentic branding is important.

A key element to success was creating an emotional connection to a landscape. One tool is the recognition through the Lasting Landscapes designation that an area has a distinct sense of place that make it a landscape worth preserving. The most compelling method is by identifying a signature property with emotional appeal, such as a heron rookery or a bat cave.

Demonstrating how the loss of a particular property would change the way people felt about their community or have a direct physical impact on the community helps establish credibility and garner support for preservation.

Pay attention to timing.

It takes time to build community support. Not only does the process have to be community based, it must also be "community paced." Change won't occur until a community is convinced the process or project is important. Involvement must come at the right time. Efforts that begin before a community sees a threat are often ignored; efforts that begin too late are often viewed as hopeless—like locking the barn door after the horse has escaped. Large-scale projects need time to develop, and individual projects must reach a critical mass before they are fully appreciated.

Collaborative work is more an art than a science. Timing is everything, and people cannot be forced into action before they are ready. Patience and vigilance help a great deal.

What you start with may not be what you end up with.

The Lasting Landscapes concept is part place, part process, and part result. As the initiative matured and evolved, it became more difficult to accurately define it. What started as a place, e.g., the Forks of Neshaminy, evolved into the means of identifying a significant place and then a methodology to ensure its permanent protection.

Celebrate successes along the way.

Because many of the Lasting Landscapes (LL) projects are comprehensive, multiyear efforts, it is important to celebrate each small success along the way. The four phases of the LL approach create natural milestones to benchmark and celebrate progress. Don't wait for the big result because it may be a long time coming. You can keep the community enthusiastic, hopeful, and engaged by celebrating each small victory.

Jeff Marshall is the vice president of resource protection at the Heritage Conservancy. Sharon Young is the coordinator for resource protection projects and lasting landscapes at the conservancy (http://www.heritageconservancy.org).

VIII. CONCLUSION

T HE CASES IN this monograph have explored the essential elements of successful collaboration. Success, like failure, leaves clues. The following are some observations about what works.

Collaboration is hard work.

Scott Peck, in his classic book *The Road Less Traveled*, opens with the line, "Life is hard." He believes that once we really understand this notion, we will be better able to live in conscious and thoughtful ways. Having a realistic perspective helps prepare you psychologically for the difficulties ahead.

So it is with collaborative work. It is hard to do. It takes tenacity, persistence, perspiration, and aspiration. There are no shortcuts. You must be fully engaged, open to others, and flexible and resilient enough to deal with the unanticipated and inevitable hurdles that come.

Do not enter into collaborative work lightly because it may change almost everything you do.

Transparency is essential.

Transparency helps create trust, and trust is essential to collaborative work. We found three areas where transparency supports collaborative work:

- *Decision making.* It is important that everyone involved in a collaborative process or initiative clearly understand the decision-making rules. The essential question that must be answered very early is, *who* is going to make *what* decisions? Participants and stakeholders must be on the same page about this *before* any decisions are made.

    Not every decision is everyone's to make, so defining people's roles in the decision-making process is essential. If the top leaders are going to make the final decisions, this must be communicated up front.

- *Data.* Information has to be shared openly with all relevant parties, and most importantly, it must be communicated in user-friendly language and images. In many organizations, information is hoarded, and only certain people have access to it. This doesn't work with collaborative processes. Information needs to be accessible and understandable.

- *Sharing people's thinking.* We found that it is helpful to have people share the thinking behind their positions. When people are able to understand the thinking of others, it creates the opportunity for dialogue and discussion. The essential skills of advocacy and inquiry are important for anyone interested in collaborative work. Advocacy essentially means seeking to be understood, putting your views forward, and promoting your perspectives and ideas. Inquiry is the skill of gaining an understanding of others. This requires openness to other ideas, authentic listening, and a willingness to be influenced by other people's thinking. Even when differences are great, when people understand *how* a person arrived at a conclusion, the possibility for discovering common ground is heightened, and areas of common ground are revealed.

"Cultural Travelers" are needed.

For collaborative work to be sustained over a long time, certain special people need to be involved throughout the process. We call them "cultural travelers." These individuals have a unique set of skills and the ability to connect with others and travel through the different "cultures" that exist within an organization and between organizations.

We generally describe culture "as the way things get done around here." It is what gets rewarded, appreciated, and sometimes punished in any organization. It includes organizational values, history, norms, and behaviors. Anyone involved in collaborative work must deeply understand the complexity of the organizational cultures in which they are working.

"Cultural travelers" have the following traits in common:

- They are deeply trusted by others, which gives them access to almost everyone. This trust is earned because they are seen as being transparent, forthright, and authentic. They are understood to be serving the common good and committed to what's best for the organization(s) and its people.

- Although these travelers are sensitive to the politics of an organization, they are never seen as political. People realize their true intentions and intuitively trust them.
- They tend to be excellent listeners. This conveys respect and value for others and gives the "traveler" access to information most people never have.
- People tend to seek these individuals out with questions and solicit their ideas, opinions, and advice. Sometimes they have high status in an organization; often they don't. They are the go-to people when things need to get done, the people you want on the team because you know their presence will matter.
- They are able to keep confidences and build bridges to others. When top leaders are "cultural travelers," their positive impact can be enormous.

Leaders need a different skill set for collaborative work.

In collaborative work, leaders must learn and exhibit a new set of skills. Some will find this approach counterintuitive in many ways because it differs greatly from the notion of leader as the one with all the answers, or the expert. With collaborative work, leaders are often asked to lead without answers because the challenges that face organizations and our society are filled with complexity, ambiguity, and nuance. For many issues, there simply are no clear answers, and leaders must trust in the skills, abilities, and aspirations of others if they are to be successful.

Leaders need to be more inclusive with decision making. They must be willing to listen to the ideas of others and be open to persuasion, able to act as facilitators and not drivers of action, and attentive to both what needs to be done and *how* it is done.

Leaders also have an important role in "holding the space" for collaborative work. Because of their position and status, they can convene stakeholders to come together to discuss, solve, dream, and implement. They can create the mechanisms and protocols for dialogue and action. They can dedicate resources and hold people accountable for results. They cannot force collaborative work, but they can support it in many ways.

Collaborative work asks leaders to take a "leap of faith" and trust in the process and the people involved. Some find this very difficult to do. You really can't mandate what matters to people; they need to psychologically buy into what needs to be done. It must be worthy of their commitment and must touch their aspirations. Telling people what to do simply doesn't work. Asking people what they want to do opens up a world of possibilities.

For any collaborative process or initiative to truly work, especially for the long haul, *internal leadership* must be committed to the process. Collaboration cannot be maintained by outsiders or consultants. Insiders have to own it. People will know early in the game if leaders are on board and will judge their own commitment by what they witness. Internal leadership and organizational champions must be visible throughout the collaborative process and not just at the beginning. They must participate in, but not dominate, the process. They must model a facilitative leadership stance and be vigilant about inclusiveness and participation.

Leaders must be able to connect with others if they are to successfully lead a collaborative effort. They must be able to touch people's hearts and minds and to garner their support and commitment over time. Leaders can connect with followers by being transparent in their word and deed, telling the truth, owning mistakes, and being authentic in their interactions.

Collaboration is not a soft approach; it is an outcome-based approach.

Results matter. That is the bottom line of any true collaborative process. You don't collaborate to make people feel good. You collaborate to get something *done*. Meaningful early wins and victories help create momentum. People need to see that their efforts are making a difference. This not only motivates them; it builds their capacity to work together in different ways. When they can see their "fingerprints" on the collaborative work, they realize that they matter, and that their participation makes a difference.

Having the "right" people at the table is essential.

In collaborative work, much thinking and energy is spent identifying *who* should be involved in the collaboration. This goes beyond the "usual suspects" list and extends to those individuals and groups that will be affected by the process, can help or hurt the process, and whose thinking and experience can add value to the process. The essential questions to ask are, what is the whole picture we need to understand, and *who* can help us understand it?

If you are working on reducing teen violence, bringing only "experts" on violence to the discussion will not solve this difficult and heart-wrenching issue. We must expand our thinking to include anyone who might have information, experience, political power, resources, or perspective that will enable us to understand the "whole." This means you need police to be involved, students to share their thoughts and perspective, and parents to help think through this complex and thorny issue. You would also need local clergy, who have huge influence with their members and deep connections to youth as well as the business community who could help create training and jobs for youth. The list is long for very different reasons.

For example, with the SCOOP summit, we had over one hundred stakeholder groups, including students, community members, the mayor, state legislators, and directors of nonprofits. Together we spent a day creating a shared picture of the future that helped change the way youth services were delivered in the city of Trenton. There were no experts, just plenty of people with passion, experience, and interest.

The key point is that usually more of us, not fewer, need to be at the table. We must rid ourselves of the notion that if we keep the "table" small, things will get done better and faster. There is very little concrete evidence that this approach works. To deal with complex and difficult issues, we need to expand our idea of who can help us think and solve these problems.

Build broad and deep.

To sustain collaboration over time (as in the PHS / Department of Recreation case study), you must engage not only top leaders but also others throughout the organization. Top leadership will not be enough, given the many senior leadership transitions that take place over time.

The commitment of top leadership is essential but is important to create ownership at all levels. For example, if a school superintendent seeks to change the curriculum throughout his or her school district, the board members have to approve it, the principals have to be convinced of its academic value, and teachers have to buy into it.

There needs to be an engagement strategy for each of these important stakeholder groups to win their commitment and ownership. Great ideas die every day because people did not think about all the important stakeholders groups that need to be involved. Mandating things from the top simply doesn't work.

Use setbacks as springboards.

In any collaborative effort, mistakes are almost inevitable. A miscommunication, someone being left out of the process, a disorganized meeting, an unanticipated conflict—the list can be endless.

How people respond to the setback is the key to moving things forward. If people get defensive or reactive, it doesn't help, and the opportunity for continued communication and connection can be lost. We must be very conscious about how we manage our mistakes.

In the PHS / Department of Recreation case study, we saw how a well-intentioned document (a memo of understanding) was received by people in the community in a negative way. The folks from PHS could have been self-righteous, but they chose not to be. They realized that the other side had a perspective *that needed to be understood.* The way they responded made all the difference because it conveyed respect and a willingness to listen.

When collaborative work becomes stalled, reaches an impasse, or a conflict emerges, *someone has to go first* in reaching out to the other parties. When someone reaches out, it conveys that this relationship and partnership matter and creates the opportunity for a better relationship to emerge. This doesn't guarantee success, but it can be very helpful.

Relationships are the "currency" of collaborative work.

People need to feel connected to each other in some way for collaboration to fulfill its potential. When people know that individuals have shared interests, values, and aspirations, they are more willing to work together. It is obviously important to have shared pictures of the future, clear goals and responsibilities, and good ways to communicate; but relationships are essential.

When people feel related to one another, they will *trust* each other. When there is a high level of trust, the possibilities are expanded. People will take risks, own their mistakes, work harder for the common good, share their strengths and limitations, and be willing to follow others.

Collaboration is democracy at its best.

At the heart of the democratic process is *civil* dialogue and debate, through which people are heard, valued, and respected. At a core level, these are the hallmarks of collaboration:

- Everybody's voice really matters.
- People feel heard.
- Different ideas are tolerated and explored.
- People can easily see how their ideas influence outcomes.
- Transparency is a guiding principle.
- Experts have their place in the process but do not drive the process.
- Leaders are inclusive and insist on full participation of others.
- Minority voices and positions have value.
- People do what's best for the common good.

With collaboration, people matter. It is democracy at its best.

INDEX

A

ASE (Automotive Service Excellence)
12

B

bat mines 77-8
Boyce, John 30
Brasko, Bill 75
Bucks County Natural Areas
Inventory 75, 78

C

Carnegie, Jon 48, 51, 58
Carroll Park 31
Center in the Park 24
City of Trenton Department of
Recreation, Natural Resources,
and Culture (DRNR&C) 7,
60, 66
collaboration
approach 86
collaborators 84-6
consensus 84
democracy 88
difficulty 83
leadership 40, 44, 85
relationships 88
transparency 83
Cooks Creek Watershed 77-8
"cultural travelers" 84-5

D

DCNR see Pennsylvania Department
of Conservation and Natural
Resources
Delaware River 79-80
DiBerardinis, Michael 6, 34-5, 37-8,
45
Durham Bat Mine 77-8
Durham Furnace and Iron Works 77

E

EIS see New Jersey Department of
Transportation: environmental
impact statement

F

Federal Highway Administration
(FHWA) 25, 50, 56
Five-Spruce Farm 75
Forks of the Neshaminy 74-6
Foster, Tyronne 29
Fox, Tom 23
FPC (Fairmount Park Commission)
23
Friends of Gorgas Park 30

G

Green, Facetta 32
Gwaltney, Doris 31

H

Heritage Conservancy 72-82

I

integrated youth services network 7,
    61-2, 87
  attitudes in 68, 70
  collaboration-enabling structures
    63-6
  collaborators 7, 63
  political power 7
  surveys 61-2
  transportation 65
  youth summits 7, 60-2, 69
ISO (International Standards
    Operation) 13

K

Kalasunas, John 28

L

large-scale collaborative planning
    process 6, 44
  communication 40-1, 44-5, 85
  internal capacity building 6, 35-6,
    38-42, 44-5
  large-scale engagement 18, 35-41
  leadership 6, 44, 48, 55, 57
Lasting Landscapes 7, 72-6, 78-82
  leadership team 73, 77, 80-1
LDP (leadership development
    program) 43

M

McCabe, Barbara 29
Musconetcong River 79

N

natural resources
  conservation 7
    community-based approach 8
    expertise 8
    model 73
    significance 7, 72
neighborhood park revitalization 5,
    22, 25, 27-8, 30
  achievements 27
  attitudes 26
  leadership 69
  partnership 5-6, 22, 27, 31
  resources 68
neighborhood parks
  capital improvements investment
    25
  neglect 22, 28
  social significance 25, 28
New Jersey Department of
    Transportation (NJDOT) 6,
    46-8, 50, 56
  environmental impact statement 6,
    47, 52, 56
North Montgomery County Area
    Vo-Tech School *see* North
    Montgomery County Technical
    Career Center
North Montgomery County Technical
    Career Center
  achievement scores 12

teachers   12
transformation   11
youth apprenticeships   13

P

Palmer, Douglas   60, 67
Partners' Roundtable   47, 49-59
Peck, Scott
Road Less Traveled, The   83
Pennsylvania Department of
      Conservation and Natural
      Resources (PDCNR)   6, 34-8,
      40, 42-5
   Action Plan   6, 34-7, 42-3, 45
Pennsylvania Department of
      Education   17
Pennsylvania Horticultural Society
      (PHS)   4-5, 22, 24, 26-7, 33,
      87-8
   Philadelphia Green Program   24,
      29-31, 33, 60
Philadelphia Department of
      Recreation (PDR)   5, 22-3,
      27-9, 32
Philadelphia Green   30
Philadelphia Parks Alliance   30, 33
Pidcock Creek   80
Princeton Packet   46

Q

Quakertown Swamp   76

R

Reilly, Joan   22, 33
Richland Township   77
Road Less Traveled, The (Peck)   83

roadway solution   6, 46-7, 49, 52, 54
   leadership   7, 48, 51, 57
   management   6, 57-8
   participative democracy   7, 49-51,
      54-7
Robins, Martin   48, 53
Route 113   79

S

Schuylkill River   79
SCOOP (Social Celebrations,
      Organizations, Opportunities
      and People)   7, 60, 62, 64-71
Stephney, Joe   23, 32

T

Trenton, New Jersey   7, 60-3, 65-7,
      69, 71, 87
Trenton School District   7

U

U.S. Route 1   46, 48, 52, 56, 59, 79

V

Vernon Park   24
vocational-technical education
      development   5, 11, 17, 19-20
   Future Search   5, 14-16, 18, 20-1
   in-class learning   13
   leadership   5, 13, 19
   on-the-job experiences   13
   opportunities   19
   parental concern   18
   state-mandated strategic planning
      5, 14, 20

W

Warwick Township 74-5
Warwick Township 1999 Open Space
    Plan 74
Weinstein, James 47
Whitman, Christine 47
William Penn Foundation 24

Y

youth service providers 7, 60-1, 64,
    66-8

PATRICK SANAGHAN AND NANCY ARONSON